# CONGO
## The Birth of a New Nation

On June 30, 1950, the Republic of the Congo was officially proclaimed—only to be plunged into bloody strife and near anarchy. Behind this tragic situation lay a history of colonial misrule. Ahead lay a drama of clashing personalities, international economic intrigue, Cold War rivalries and one of the U.N.'s most difficult challenges as it was called upon to restore order. Written with understanding and objectivity, *Congo* offers vital insight into the handicaps faced by emerging nations in a world swept by the winds of change.

# Books by Jules Archer

AFRICAN FIREBRAND: Kenyatta of Kenya

ANGRY ABOLITIONIST: William Lloyd Garrison

BATTLEFIELD PRESIDENT: Dwight D. Eisenhower

COLOSSUS OF EUROPE: Metternich

CONGO: The Birth of a New Nation

FIGHTING JOURNALIST: Horace Greeley

FRONT-LINE GENERAL: Douglas MacArthur

MAN OF STEEL: Joseph Stalin

RED REBEL: Tito of Yugoslavia

SCIENCE EXPLORER: Roy Chapman Andrews

TWENTIETH CENTURY CAESAR: Benito Mussolini

WORLD CITIZEN: Woodrow Wilson

# *CONGO*
## THE BIRTH OF A NEW NATION

## by Jules Archer

*map-photographs*

# JULIAN MESSNER    NEW YORK

Published simultaneously in the United States and Canada by
Julian Messner, a division of Simon & Schuster, Inc.,
1 West 39 Street, New York, N. Y. 10018. All rights reserved.

To

Dr. Vincent Russo
for his selfless dedication
to the grateful community of
Pine Plains, N.Y.

*Map by William Jaber*
*All photographs courtesy United Nations*

Printed in the United States of America

ISBN 0-671-32302-4 Cloth Trade
0-671-32303-2 MCE

Library of Congress Catalog Card No. 73-123174

# Contents

# Contents

# 1
# Freedom or Anarchy?

THE CONGOLESE COULD scarcely believe it. After almost a century of colonial rule, the Belgians had agreed to hand the country back to its people. On June 30, 1960, the sunbaked streets of Leopoldville, the capital, overflowed with jubilant Africans celebrating the birth of their freedom.

To mark the historic transfer of power from white Belgians to black Congolese, King Baudoin himself spoke at the Independence Day ceremonies. Paying homage to the early Belgian colonizers, he praised especially his ancestor King Leopold II as a kind, generous humanitarian who had brought civilization to the Congo. Congolese were reminded of all the sacrifices that Belgium had made to prepare them for this great day, when they were becoming masters of their own fate.

On the speaker's platform was a lean, spectacled African in Western clothes who grew increasingly angry as he listened. When the Prime Minister of the new Democratic Republic of the Congo was called upon to offer a protocol reply to the King's address, he rose and strode stiffly to the lectern. Hundreds of foreign dignitaries applauded politely.

7

Fiercely nationalistic Patrice Lumumba flung aside his prepared speech and delivered a blistering denunciation of Belgian colonialism that stunned his listeners.

"We have known tiring labor," he shouted furiously, "exacted in exchange for salary which did not allow us to satisfy our hunger, to clothe and lodge ourselves decently or to raise our children like loved beings! We have known ironies, insults, blows which we had to endure morning, noon and night because we were Negroes! The law was never the same, depending on whether it concerned a white or a Negro; accommodating for one group, it was cruel and inhuman for the other."

Outraged Belgian officials in the audience began storming out. Lumumba watched them go derisively.

"We have known that there were magnificent houses for the whites in the cities and tumbledown straw huts for the Negroes; that a Negro was not admitted in movie houses or restaurants or stores labeled 'European'; that a Negro traveled in the hulls of riverboats at the feet of the white in his first-class cabin. Who will forget, finally, the fusillades where so many of our brothers perished, or the prisons where all those were brutally flung who no longer wished to submit to the regime of a law of oppression and exploitation which the colonists had made a tool of their domination?"

Shaken, King Baudoin stalked off the podium. Many foreign visitors, indignant at Lumumba's breach of protocol, followed the Belgians out of the ceremony. Sobered by this exodus and cooler with the bitterness out of his system, Lumumba sought to make amends with a halfhearted tribute.

"Even Belgium, who after all understands the meaning of history, has not tried to oppose our independence further," he conceded, "and is ready to give us her help and her friendship; and a treaty with this understanding has been signed between our two equal and independent countries."

Hours later the new Congo President, Joseph Kasavubu, rebuked him angrily for his imprudent outburst. What had Lumumba hoped to gain by raking up old grievances after the Belgians had agreed to help make the new Congo Republic work? Was he aware that King Baudoin and many foreign diplomats were so incensed that they were planning to leave the Congo at once? Did he realize that his inflammatory speech had stirred up unrest on the mobbed streets of Leopoldville?

The fault, Lumumba protested, lay with King Baudoin for having misrepresented the quality of Belgian rule in a smug speech. How *dare* Baudoin ignore the suffering and humiliation of the Congolese under colonialism! Could Lumumba be expected to tolerate such a crude display of racial arrogance?

But pragmatic reflection restored his perspective. Later that same day, in the presence of the King, he sought to retrieve his diplomatic gaffe with a small speech in which he politely thanked Belgium for all it had done for the Congo, and for voluntarily offering independence.

Lumumba's concession mollified the Belgians somewhat, but had little effect in calming down his overexcited countrymen. As the day wore on, tribal rivalries began to surface above the celebration in the nation's capital.

National unity was, at best, a fragile concept among thirteen and a half million Congolese fragmented into 200 tribes, each convinced that its own way of life was the ideal model for the whole country. The tragic truth about independence was that there was really no "Democratic Republic of the

Congo"—only a flimsy amalgamation of 200 different ethnic groups with sharply conflicting traditions and goals.

All were included in the concept called "the Congo" only because early white colonists had constructed an arbitrary country out of adjacent tribes, and parts of tribes, that they dominated and controlled. The Congo was no more an indigenous country than one that might be put together from the United States, Mexico and adjacent corners of Canada, Guatemala, Honduras, Nicaragua, Costa Rica, El Salvador, Panama and Colombia. The Congo had only one unifying factor— black skins.

The thrust for an independent Congo had come about when King Baudoin, in 1955, had felt compelled to decree that blacks in Belgium's principal colony should be allowed to "share in the country's government, each according to his own quality and capacity." This concession had led to the education of a few thousand Congolese by 1958.

This Congolese elite, awarded citizenship and minor civil service jobs, were called *evolués* (blacks who had evolved into the privileges of citizenship through education). Some were relatively content with the degree of well-being they had achieved as white-collar workers.

But most felt that their privileges did not compensate for enduring a racist colonialism that prevented them from winning deserved major posts. Seeking a more equitable distribution of power, they mounted a protest that eventually impelled the Belgian Government to consent to national elections that would culminate in freedom for the Congo.

Ambitious candidates in the election campaign of spring, 1960, did not hesitate to make demagogic promises about what independence would bring to the Congolese. Some toured

the countryside pledging that the new republic would turn
over to black men all white men's jobs, houses, cars and personal property. To the average Congolese, a wife and daughter came under the heading of a man's "property."

Tribal candidates assured constituents that after independence, they would provide thousands of high-paying government jobs. Other notions of what Independence Day would
bring were fostered by witch doctors like those at Kandale,
where Congolese were told to bury boxes of stones, which
would be turned to gold when the Congo was freed. Dead
relatives would also then be resurrected to join their families.

Within 24 hours of the proclamation of a Congo Republic,
the so-called nation began to splinter apart in tribal conflict.
The Force Publique, a native army organized by the Belgians,
were compelled to arrest hundreds of Congolese and jail 93.
Ancient tribal hatreds, sparked by African beer, were only
part of the trouble caused by independence celebrations.

Congolese were also rapidly disillusioned when their
naïve expectations of independence failed to materialize. No
Belgian officials had taken the trouble to tour the country
explaining what changes they might realistically anticipate.

"Now I can do anything I want!" one villager asserted
jubilantly. Another announced, "No more taxes now! Plenty
to eat, clothes for everyone, a car and home for every
family!" One tribal chief promised, "Everyone can now get
all the money he wants because our Government will print
as much as is needed." His people besieged banks demanding
money.

"What is independence?" one Congolese asked a Belgian.
"Will it come in a package? Can I unwrap it right away?"

Some Congolese considered independence to mean that

Belgians would have to say hello and shake hands with them.
Others said it meant that all Belgians were to leave the Congo
at once.

There was widespread bitterness when Independence Day
came and went with no fulfillment of these fanciful expectations. It did not help matters that the few government jobs
available went to close friends and relatives of ministers and
tribal chiefs. Thousands of Congolese who had worked hard
for electoral candidates were chagrined. Preferences shown
one tribe over another caused old tribal rivalries to seethe.

Matters worsened when communications and liaison between the new Central Government and local administrators
broke down. Teachers, police, officials and troops grew furious
as payrolls failed to arrive and inquiries were ignored.

On Independence Day there were over 8,200 white Belgians
in important administrative posts, but many were preparing
to leave, seeing no future in a country controlled by Africans.
No black men had been trained to replace them. Except for
three in the upper echelons of civil service, not a single Congolese held a position higher than that of a minor clerk.
There was not one African military officer, doctor, engineer
or lawyer. The entire Congo could boast of a total of only 20
black university graduates.

Unprepared for freedom, the new Republic quickly fell
into chaos. Strikes broke out in the country's largest shipping
firm, as well as among Coquilhatville's government clerks and
Leopoldville's postal workers. Irresponsible election campaign promises of huge wage raises had failed to materialize,
but the new bureaucrats had swiftly voted themselves annual
salaries of up to $30,000. They had inflamed popular opinion

further by flaunting their new opulence, riding around grandly in new Cadillacs.

On July 4, 1960, soldiers stationed in Equator Province
were ordered to disperse demonstrations supporting the
strikers in Coquilhatville. Angry tribesmen responded by
unleashing a shower of arrows at the troops. Opening fire,
the Force Publique killed nine Africans and wounded many
others.

When independence dawned, the Congo's security forces
consisted of a thousand white officers and 24,000 illiterate
black enlisted men who served away from their own villages
to assure that tribal loyalty would not interfere with obedience to orders.

A few months before independence, spokesmen for Africans in the Force Publique had addressed a protest to the
Belgian Governor General: "Our officers live like Americans
in big modern houses. They are arrogant and must always
be the master. All this is because they are white. All African
soldiers today have one desire: to fill the posts of command,
to earn a decent salary and to end discrimination in the Force.
If you have not before June 30 taken the necessary steps,
independence will be a mockery."

But after Independence Day, Lumumba flatly declared that
he had no intention of being stampeded by pressure from
Africans in the Force Publique. Angry noncommissioned officers and enlisted men promptly staged a protest rally at
the principal staging area, Camp Leopold II in Leopoldville.

Next morning the Belgian general Emile Janssens called a
meeting of all NCOs. In large chalk letters he wrote on the
camp bulletin board "BEFORE INDEPENDENCE=AFTER
INDEPENDENCE." Independence was purely a civilian

matter, he informed his black troops coldly. They would continue to render absolute obedience to their officers or face court-martial.

The indignant NCOs mutinied, with the full support of the camp's six dollar-a-month privates. Janssens at once sent for troops from Camp Hardy at Thysville, 95 miles south of Leopoldville. But when white officers there tried to assemble a convoy, their black troops also mutinied. Some officers were beaten, and others were threatened with bayonets.

"*We* are the masters now!" one black private shouted.

Thousands of Camp Leopold's mutineers poured into Leopoldville, assaulting Europeans, smashing stores and looting. Some NCOs led invasions of Parliament and government buildings, demanding Lumumba's resignation, the ousting of Belgian advisers from the Government, the firing of General Janssens and the replacement of all white Army officers by Africans.

The rioting was even more frenzied in Thysville. Drunken troops committed brutal outrages against Belgian and foreign civilians. Beaten with gun stocks, white men were told, "This is what independence means!" Shoeless victims were forced to flatten rolls of barbed wire with their bare feet. Some wives of white officers were seized and raped.

By July 6, Lumumba was forced to conciliate the mutineers. He agreed to replace all white Belgian officers with Congolese NCOs and to promote every member of the force one grade, making the Congo Army the only one in the world without a single private. General Janssens was fired and replaced by Victor Lundula, a former sergeant major, under President Kasavubu as Commander-in-Chief. Lumumba exon-

14

erated the mutineers, blaming all the trouble on the racism of Belgian officers and other "enemies of our independence."

But the social explosions touched off by the mutiny were so volatile that they were not easily brought under control. Outbreaks of mutiny, rape and assaults swept through the Congo like a tidal wave of unleashed violence.

In the capital 700 African police put their five white commissioners under arrest. In Elizabethville (Katanga Province) mutineers shot two Belgian officers and four white civilians. Mutiny spread to Matadi (Leopoldville Province), Luluabourg (Kasai Province), Stanleyville (Oriental Province) and other key cities. Frightened whites began heading for the Congo's borders by car, plane and riverboat and on foot.

Panicky Europeans jamming into Ndjili airport unloaded their property at a fraction of its value to well-dressed Africans soliciting them in the departure lounge with bags of money. The flight of the whites infuriated the mutineers, who became even more menacing and violent. The chaos worsened with outbreaks of tribal warfare. Unchecked by the mutinous Force Publique, fighting flared in Kasai Province between the Baluba and Bena Lulua. Over 200 houses went up in flames in Luluabourg.

"The Europeans at Sonankulu were thrown into Thysville prison," charged a Belgian Government report. "They were humiliated, stripped naked, people spat in their faces; they were beaten and ridiculed. At Luluabourg . . . families that did not find safety were often the victims of serious outrages. A European civilian was shot down. Two families, each with several children, were molested and beaten. Mrs. Z. was raped at gunpoint in her home by two policemen. . . . Other

15

women, including an old lady, were stripped, molested and publicly humiliated." Other unspeakable atrocities were alleged.

On July 6, Moise Tshombe, Premier of Katanga, the Congo's richest and most important province, flew to Leopoldville for a confrontation with Kasavubu and Lumumba. As head of CONAKAT, the political party friendliest to Belgian interests, Tshombe insisted that the new Central Government permit the Belgians to restore order by flying troops into the two large Congo bases they had been allowed to retain by treaty.

Lumumba and Kasavubu angrily refused. Did Tshombe want to give the world the impression that the new republic was helpless to control its own affairs? And on the very day that the U.N. Security Council was unanimously recommending the admission of the Congo to membership in the U.N.?

When he returned to Katanga, Tshombe defied Lumumba and Kasavubu and called publicly for intervention by Belgian troops to put down mutineers in the southern Congo.

On July 8, a rumor flashed around Leopoldville that the mutineers were marching on the city, attacking every white woman who fell into their hands. Europeans fled from their homes in the middle of the night. Belgian youths ran through the streets brandishing guns and yelling, "Let us fight till we die!" The distant sound of a rifle shot—or car backfire—was enough to cause a whole district to panic and seek to flee across the Congo River to the safety of Brazzaville, capital of a similarly named but independent Republic of Congo, formerly a French possession.

"Shouting, screaming, crying, the refugees fled into nearby buildings, behind trees and rocks, any hiding place they could find," reported UPI correspondent George Sibera. "Others, zigzagging and looking back fearfully, ran to the river . . . to mob the ferry dock. . . . The refugees failed to calm down until they actually had entered Brazzaville waters. . . . But I did not hear a single shot." In a single night 3,000 to 4,000 Belgians fled the Congo in hysteria, leaving behind thousands of abandoned cars.

One Associated Press reporter found that some mutineer leaders, far from seeking to assault Belgians, were only trying to stem their exodus. Lumumba had convinced them that without the help of Belgian technicians, untrained and inexperienced Congolese could not operate the economy.

Lumumba and Kasavubu were less successful in restraining mutineers in Matadi and Stanleyville, where hundreds of whites were seized, stripped, roped together, beaten by gun butts, kicked, spat at and humiliated. Some were tortured at the insistence of enraged blacks brutalized by Belgian rule. Nuns had their robes torn and were outraged. Men wounded by mutineers' bullets were denied medical treatment and died.

By July 9, Belgium's Sabena Airlines was compelled to cancel all scheduled flights in order to operate an airlift for thousands of desperate refugees. Two U.S. planes arrived in Leopoldville to evacuate all American personnel in the Congo. The mass exodus of whites intensified chaos everywhere.

Hundreds of thousands of Congolese were left without jobs or money. A food shortage developed. A scarcity of doctors and nurses increased the danger of epidemics. More and more tribes added to the turmoil by reverting to tribal warfare.

Acting under Tshombe's authorization, the Belgian Government moved to protect its nationals. Belgian troops were rushed to its Congo bases as Tshombe strengthened their hand by threatening to call for help from British Rhodesia.

The angered Congo Cabinet, in Lumumba's absence, asked the United States for military help. President Dwight D. Eisenhower cautiously refused. He was willing to give economic aid to the new Congo Republic, but feared that sending troops might extend the Cold War with the Soviet Union to Africa. He recommended instead that the Congo Republic appeal to the U.N. for help in maintaining its security.

In Katanga, meanwhile, Belgium's giant mining company, Union Miniere, closed down its mines and evacuated its white employees. Belgian troops rounded up and disarmed mutinous Force Publique units. Paratroops were dropped into Kongolo to rescue white inhabitants. About 100 troops, mostly Force Publique Africans, were killed in the fighting that restored order to Katanga.

An infuriated Lumumba denounced Belgium's use of troops as a violation of Congo sovereignty. Brussels replied that since its citizens had been mistreated, looted, raped and murdered, it had a clear right under international law to intervene to protect its nationals.

Tshombe appointed a Belgian major to reorganize the Force Publique in Katanga. Non-Katangan soldiers were disarmed and sent home. The last straw for Lumumba came when Belgian paratroops flew into Leopoldville airport and captured it. He ordered the Force Publique to counterattack, and compelled the Belgians to retreat southwest to Matadi.

Here the paratroops set the waterfront ablaze, destroying the new republic's entire gas supply, and massacred Africans indiscriminately. The news infuriated Congolese everywhere. At Thysville a soldier yelled at a Belgian official "There will be as many European corpses in Thysville as African corpses in Matadi!" In the bitter bloodshed that followed, over 50

Belgians were killed and up to a thousand Belgian women were carnally attacked.

By the end of the first week of the Force Publique mutiny, at least 30,000 Belgians had fled the Congo.

On July 11, 1960, in the midst of the chaos, Moise Tshombe suddenly proclaimed the secession of the wealthy, all-important Province of Katanga. He requested and won continuation of independent Belgian financial, technical and military aid.

The imminent collapse of the new republic of the Congo, only eleven days after its hopeful inception, seemed inevitable. And if the Congo fell, what hope could there be for more less developed African nations seeking to shake off the chains of colonialism for the bright promise of freedom?

Why had independence led so swiftly to disaster?

# 2
# Kings, Slaves and Explorers

THE CONGO, ONE-THIRD THE SIZE of the United States with over 14 million people, is one of the most important countries in Africa. It possesses a highly developed network of roads and riverways for extracting its great natural resources, and occupies a strategic position in the heart of the continent.

When it won independence from Brussels in 1960, the birth pains of the new republic were worsened by a Cold War struggle between the Soviet Union and the United States to control it, not merely for commercial gain but also as the keystone of an African sphere of influence.

The turmoil of the Congo in the sixties underscored the perils of turning loose a colony unprepared for freedom. In just two short weeks of life, the chaotic republic fell into a crisis that threatened the very survival of the United Nations and raised the grim specter of a nuclear world war. When the troubles in the Congo became the troubles of the whole world, people everywhere were stunned by the realization of how distances between nations had shrunk, with tremors in Leopoldville quickly felt in New York, Brussels, Moscow, and Bombay.

The Congo's impact upon the world, however, was nothing new. Far from being some obscure country that had rarely been heard of until it shook off Belgian colonialism, the Congo has had a long and tragic history that often compelled world attention and concern.

The earliest inhabitants of the Congo were pygmies, thought to have arrived during the Paleolithic era. They are mentioned in the writings of Homer, Herodotus, and Aristotle. Pressed back into the dense forest regions by Bantu migrants from the northwest, they survived by hunting and gathering food. Their descendants, now numbering only 80,000, live the same way.

One of the oldest kingdoms in all Africa developed in what is now Kasai Province. As early as A.D. 500 the first Bakuba kings developed a highly sophisticated society. The Bakubas decorated and carved their houses, drums, cups, vases and cosmetic boxes, many examples of which are now prized as relics of classic African art.

In the 16th century King Shamba Bolongongo, who maintained court artists, was distressed by the persistence of tribal wars. He forbade his subjects, expert knife-throwers feared as "the lightning people," the use of all weapons. A sculpture of this early African pacifist survives today as the oldest work of art in central Africa.

Modern Bakubas remain proudly conscious of their ancient heritage. At the court of Nyimi one must approach the chief's throne only indirectly, through a carefully prescribed and guarded labyrinth, not only for the chief's protection but also to impress upon callers the exalted station of a monarch descended from 15 centuries of Bakuba royalty.

Another famous African empire was the Bakongo Kingdom, founded at the end of the 13th century by Bantu hunters, largely in what became Leopoldville Province. The country was divided into provinces and districts governed by appointed chiefs and, in a few cases, elected officials. The Bakongo practiced the arts of making pottery and casting metal; raised pigs, sheep and goats; grew fruits, vegetables and grains; and wove cloth from bark so well that early Portuguese explorers used it for sails.

The Congo first came to European attention eight years before Columbus discovered America. In search of an eastward route to the Indies, Portugal's Prince Henry the Navigator ordered exploration of the African coast. In 1484 mariner Diego Cão arrived at the mouth of the Congo River. Finding the Bakongo kingdom there under Nzinga Ntinu, Diego Cão at first thought he had found the mythical realm of Prester John, where great wealth was supposed to be so generously divided that there were no poor, thieves or misers.

Nzinga Ntinu was even more impressed with his Portuguese visitors than they with him, and he decided to detain them for a unique ransom. His ambassadors went to Lisbon to negotiate the price: technical assistance for the Bakongo. King John II agreed and dispatched masons, carpenters, farmers and missionaries to the court of Nzinga Ntinu.

Releasing the hostages, the King of the Bakongo entered into an alliance with the King of Portugal under which the Portuguese were allowed to take slaves for their plantations in Brazil. Ambassadors were exchanged, and young tribal noblemen were sent to Lisbon for instruction as dukes and earls. In 1491 Nzinga Ntinu converted the Bakongo to Catholicism.

During the reign of his son Affonso I, thousands of Portuguese businessmen and missionaries immigrated to the Congo, building trading posts, churches, schools and courts. A humane man, Affonso was shocked to find that the Portuguese criminal code, recommended to him as a model, prescribed savage penalties for trivial offenses. "What is the penalty in Portugal," he asked Lisbon's ambassador dryly, "for anyone who dares put his feet on the ground?"

He grew increasingly upset by Portuguese expeditions under half-caste traders that brutally raided Bakongo villages to ship "black-ivory" overseas from the port of Mpinda on the Congo River. He protested angrily to both Lisbon and Rome against the exploitation of his kingdom as a slave mine.

But it was not until 1660 that the Bakongo rose against Portugal, which sent troops to crush the revolt. The Portuguese gradually lost their monopoly on the slave trade, however, as French, British and Dutch rivals sought to profit from the thriving demand for slaves in America.

Ironically, in the same year that white Americans gathered in Philadelphia to declare their freedom from British tyranny, over 100,000 black Africans were shipped into slavery, many to plantations owned by America's founding fathers. A third of them had been kidnapped in the Congo and Angola.

Between the 15th and 19th centuries European ships carried away an estimated 30,000,000 Congolese slaves—more than twice the country's population today.

Although Portugal had crushed the Bakongo revolt, the Lisbon court soon decided that the Congo was no longer safe or profitable, and shifted its interest and resources to adjacent Angola. When its missionaries and traders left, the bitter Bakongo repudiated Christianity as a cloak for enslavement. The Belgians, arriving in the Congo late in the 19th century, found that the churches had declined into moss-covered ruins. The Bakongo kingdom itself, unable to recover from military defeat, had fallen into decay, becoming only a loose scattering of village tribes.

There were two other major Congo kingdoms besides the Bakuba and the Bakongo. These occupied rival realms in what is now the Province of Katanga. The Baluba empire, founded in the 15th century, lasted for 200 years. It went into decline when weakened by Portuguese and Arab slave raids, and lost its dominance in tribal wars with the Lunda.

As the slavers pressed deeper into the Congo, about 15 million blacks escaped by retreating into the jungles. Starvation forced many into cannibalism for survival. They were saved from possible total extermination by growing world indignation, spread by books and newspapers, over the horrors of the traffic in human flesh.

By 1807 the slave trade was outlawed in Great Britain, and by 1833 was abolished in all its colonies. Portugal followed suit in 1835, France in 1848. Even so, the slave trade persisted as a smuggling operation. By 1850 the estuary of the Congo River was still lined with warehouses from which slaves were regularly bought and exported.

The Arabs continued an open, barbarous slave trade supplying the Middle East from Indian Ocean ports. At the height of their raids they shipped out about 70,000 slaves a year. Tens of thousands more perished in the agonizing trek in chains from the east Congo to the coast. One half-breed Arab slaver, Tippo-Tip, became so rich and powerful that he made himself master of a huge area of the Congo. Europeans seeking to pass through it had to bribe him for permission.

The opening of the Congo by the slavers brought Europeans

with a different mission—scientific discovery. Some came searching the interior for the sources of the Nile. A hardy lot, the explorers were nevertheless often shaken by the gruesome sights they saw on their expeditions.

In 1816 a British explorer named Tuckey led an expedition up the 2,735-mile Congo River that sprawled through the country like a huge, twisting tree snake. In some remote villages he found all the inhabitants lying on the earth, living skeletons starved and diseased, waiting for death. Throughout the Congo malaria, leprosy, trypanosomiasis and tropical ulcers went untreated except by witch doctors. Tuckey and 17 others on the expedition died of tropical fever.

In 1870 Dr. David Livingstone, an English missionary-explorer, discovered Lake Moero in the Katanga region. He was horrified at the massacres of blacks he saw committed by brutal Arab slave merchants working for Tippo-Tip.

The explorer who penetrated most deeply into the Congo was Henry Morton Stanley, an English-born newspaper reporter working for James Gordon Bennett's *New York Herald*. When Livingstone was reported missing, Bennett sent Stanley in search of him as a circulation-building stunt.

"No matter how much it costs," Bennett ordered, "find and help Livingstone!" Stanley's quest through the Congo became an adventure classic. In 999 days of beating his way through jungles no white man had ever penetrated before, he had battles with hostile Africans, suppressed several mutinies in his expedition and survived poisonous spiders, scorpions, crocodiles, tree snakes and tropical disease.

He finally located the object of his search at Ujiji on November 10, 1871, uttering that famous line, "Dr. Livingstone, I presume?" Livingstone was amazed not only at learning that an expedition had been sent to find him (he didn't consider himself lost) but also at the lavishness of Stanley's caravan. Stanley joined him on explorations for four months, then made his way back to the coast. What he had seen greatly impressed Stanley with the Congo's commercial possibilities.

"The Congo River," he predicted, "will be the grand highway of commerce in West Central Africa."

His enthusiasm was shared by British explorer Lovett Cameron, who had led a Royal Geographical Society expedition through the Congo for two and a half years. In January, 1876, he sent back glowing reports extolling the healthy climate, beautiful scenery and deposits of coal, iron, gold and copper in Katanga. Cameron also marveled at the rich agricultural crops and harvests of wild rubber he had seen on his journey.

The reports of Stanley and Cameron greatly intrigued the King of the Belgians, Leopold II. A born empire-builder, Leopold began thinking of colonizing the region. Hadn't little England grown great and rich through colonization? Why not little Belgium? But other countries were already rushing expeditions to the Congo to plant flags and claim boundaries.

They began quarreling over claims, even to the point of war threats. Then Leopold had a brilliant inspiration.

He knew that Europe did not really want to go to war over the Congo. But each nation was reluctant to withdraw its claims for fear that others would grab the spoils. Leopold evolved a clever scheme to get them all to agree to let *him* administer the Congo as a "noble trust for all civilization." As a humanitarian cloak for exploitation, he took for his aim a sacred mission to wipe out the slave trade.

The explorers had sent home horrifying accounts of slavery, particularly as practiced by the Arab slave traders. Livingstone had reported watching a party of slavers come into a marketplace at Nyangwe and begin shooting the women, hundreds of whom were killed or drowned trying to escape.

"I had the impression that I was in hell," wrote the anguished missionary. "My first impulse was to pistol the murderers, but I was helpless." Cameron also sent back reports of murders and atrocities committed by the Arab slavers, whose long caravans he had encountered on his travels.

Leopold knew that world opinion would favor his plan to move into the Congo in the name of suppressing the slave trade. His own people, too thrifty to approve of spending vast sums for a colonial adventure, would support an appeal to their Christian compassion. Belgian missionaries would follow Belgian troops. Belgian businessmen would follow the clergy.

So Leopold invited Britain, Portugal, France, Italy, Germany, Austria-Hungary and Russia to a Brussels Geographic Conference on September 12, 1876. Urging these powers to neutralize the Congo by turning it into an "International Africa Association" (A.I.A.), he pointed out that the abolition of the shameful slave trade was assured if they all joined forces to suppress it. The A.I.A. would also, of course, open up the Congo to international commerce for the benefit of all.

Exploratory expeditions would be organized first to establish hospitals and scientific camps, "preparing the Congo for civilization." The greater part of the Congo basin, from the hot flat forest country of the north to the cool high savannahs of the south, was still unexplored and unmapped.

"To open to civilization the only area of our globe to which it has not yet penetrated," Leopold said loftily, "constitutes a Crusade worthy of this century of progress, and I am delighted to note how deeply public opinion approves."

To his joy the conference agreed to designate him personal custodian of the Congo, making him head of a "Congo Free State" as well as King of Belgium. This did not make the Congo a Belgian colony, but simply gave Leopold an extra job he could use for his personal enrichment. He did not hesitate to lay out private funds for the new A.I.A., knowing that he would soon be repaid a thousandfold.

Meanwhile, Stanley had returned to the Congo seeking to solve geographical problems left undetermined at Livingstone's death in 1873. This time he started from the east coast and proved that the Lualaba River, only partially explored by Livingstone and Cameron, joined the Congo River, making it one huge water passage curving through the Congo like a bend-high horseshoe. Of three white men who accompanied him on this hazardous, grueling journey, all died.

Stanley emerged from his second expedition on August 10, 1877, firmly convinced that "the Congo natives are susceptible of civilization and the Congo basin is rich enough to repay exploitation." Returning to his native England rather than America, he sought to win industrial backing for a development project.

The British, despite their consent to Leopold's custodianship of the Congo through the A.I.A., had not really given up their own colonial ambitions in the region. Cecil Rhodes, the great British empire-builder, wanted Katanga, not only for its rich copper deposits but also for the railway he hoped to build from Egypt to the Cape of Good Hope.

But the British were dubious that a man of Stanley's temperament was diplomat enough to entrust with the execution of their aims in Africa. He had, after all, been involved in 32 battles with natives during his second expedition.

Leopold was kept apprised of these secret negotiations through the espionage of Baron Solvyns, his ambassador to London, who suggested that he make a deal with Stanley.

The King's reply was cynically candid.

"I do not want to risk either offending the English or losing a fine chance to secure for use a slice of this magnificent African cake," he wrote. "If I like Stanley I will raise money for him to arrange the thorough exploitation of some of the territories on the Congo and its tributaries, and to found posts there. As circumstances allow, I shall try to transform these posts into something like Belgian establishments, or into water or land stations which will be ours."

He added, "I think that if I entrusted Stanley publicly with the job of taking over part of Africa in my own name, the English would stop me. If I consult them, they will again try to stop me. So I think that at first I shall give Stanley an exploring job which will not offend anybody, and will provide us with some posts down in that region and with a high command for them which we can develop when Europe and Africa can have got used to our 'pretensions' on the Congo."

It was scarcely surprising that almost a century later Patrice Lumumba blew up at King Baudoin for lauding his ancestor Leopold as a philanthropic benefactor of the Congo.

In June, 1878, Leopold invited Stanley to Brussels and proposed that he return to the Congo to win over tribal chiefs and establish a chain of trading posts for the A.I.A. The King planned to have these posts slide unobtrusively under his personal control later, when Europe wouldn't notice.

He was unperturbed by Stanley's dubious reputation among

explorers and missionaries because of the adventurer's habit of "bargaining" at gunpoint, and insistence upon sybaritic comfort on his expeditions. Leopold did not particularly care how Stanley got results so long as he got them. The explorer had demonstrated the aggressive energy to blaze his way through a hostile land that had killed lesser men.

Under the auspices of a "Survey Committee for the Upper Congo" and accompanied by a staff of Belgian officers, Stanley left once more for Africa. Within three years he had established 30 posts and built a road through the jungle. Congolese carried on their backs parts of the first steamers assembled and launched on the Upper Congo River. Stanley concluded treaties with river chiefs that gave Leopold exploitation rights to their territories, in exchange for gin, bits of cloth and discarded uniforms.

He was unable to reach the north shore of the Upper Congo River before the French, however, and Savorgnan de Brazza claimed that region as the French Congo. On the south shore, opposite Brazzaville, Stanley founded Leopoldville.

Leopold let the fictitious committee he had used to hire Stanley die quietly. In its place he created the International Congo Association (A.I.C.), whose blue flag with gold star represented nobody except Leopold himself.

"Care must be taken," he cautioned Colonel Maximilian Strauch, his secretary-general of the A.I.A., "not to let it be obvious that the A.I.C. and the A.I.A. are two different things. The public doesn't grasp this."

When Stanley was sent back to the Congo in 1883 to continue sweeping the Congo into Leopold's pocket, the King told Strauch, "The terms of the treaties Stanley has made with native chiefs do not satisfy me. There must at least be added an article to the effect that they delegate to us their sovereign rights over the territories. The treaties must be as brief as possible and . . . must grant us everything."

Stanley dutifully concluded new treaties with 500 Congo chiefs, and established a network of 40 posts covering almost half of the present-day Congo. These posts made it possible for expeditions to travel the full length of the Congo basin from the Atlantic, bypassing rapids and falls that impeded continuous navigation of the river. With five steamers operating on Stanley Pool, the Congo was ready for milking.

It was essential to Leopold's scheme that Europe's powers not realize that their authorized International African Association (A.I.A.) had been dumped in the signing of the native treaties, replaced by the similar-sounding International Congo Association (A.I.C.), which was his own creature. How could he be sure that his sordid plot would not be noticed or challenged? Then he had a brilliant idea.

What if he could hoodwink America into blessing it?

# 3
# Leopold's Chamber of Horrors

HE FLATTERED THE AMERICAN CONSUL in Brussels, Henry S. Sanford, into helping him draft a letter to Washington emphasizing trading opportunities for the United States in the Congo, and asking for recognition of the A.I.C. Sanford even took the letter to President Chester A. Arthur himself.

Arthur was gulled into praising the accomplishments of the A.I.C in the Congo, observing ineptly that " it does not aim at permanent political control." In April, 1884, the United States recognized the A.I.C. as a sovereign state. The delighted Leopold was able to persuade 13 European powers attending a Berlin Conference in November to follow America's example.

The General Act of Berlin, signed in February, 1885, guaranteed to all signatories freedom of commerce and navigation in the Congo, as well as free trade without favoritism. The slave trade was to be abolished; alcohol was to be kept away from the natives; Congolese living conditions and spiritual well-being were to be improved.

On April 30, 1885, the Belgian Parliament authorized Leopold as sovereign of the new Congo Free State. The Parliament, more aware of their King's true nature than the rest of the world, prudently made it clear that the Congo was the "exclusively personal" enterprise of Leopold, and that Belgium itself bore no responsibility for it.

"We are launching one of the greatest civilizing and humanitarian crusades in history," Leopold announced grandly as he crowned himself absolute ruler of a vast territory of nearly a million square miles, "to destroy the slave trade in the Congo!"

Whenever the financial strain of developing the Congo became too great, he was granted loans from the Belgian treasury. He also won grudging permission from the Berlin Conference powers to impose a 10 per cent tariff on all Congo commerce. But his most adroit move was to designate all unoccupied land "state property." From 1891 on traders had to buy most supplies of ivory, rubber and palm oil through a virtual monopoly operated by government agents.

And Leopold was the Government. His plan, he confided to a trusted aide, was "absolute ownership, uncontested, of the Congo and its riches." Newspapermen visiting the Congo discovered and began exposing his schemes.

"Leopold declared all the rubber in the country the property of the 'state,' " charged American correspondent Richard Harding Davis, "and then, to make sure that the natives would work it, ordered that taxes be paid in rubber. If, once a month, each village did not bring in so many baskets of rubber, the King's cannibal soldiers raided it, carried off the women as hostages and made prisoners of the men, or killed and ate them. For every kilo of rubber brought in in excess of the quota the King's agent was paid a commission. . . . If he obtained it 'cheaply' or for nothing—that is, by taking hostages, making prisoners or by torture—so much greater his fortune, so much richer Leopold."

Such exposés created a sensation in America and Europe.

Belgians grew increasingly disturbed and eventually hostile toward Leopold's private empire. He strove to appease them by using part of his profits for a program of Belgian public works. Belgian businessmen were seduced by being allowed to share in the wealth extracted from the Congo.

He sought to mollify church outrage by inviting Belgian, British, American and Swedish missionaries to operate the clinics and schools of the Congo. And he ordered military campaigns against Arab slave traders by a Belgian-led Congolese Army otherwise used for "pacification."

When Tippo-Tip proved too powerful to attack, Stanley was authorized to make an astonishing deal. The Congo Free State appointed the infamous slave trader as Governor of Stanleyville at $150 a month, ruling the eastern Congo with the pledge to outlaw the slave traffic in the region under his control. His vassals were infuriated. Three years later they broke his power and forced Tippo-Tip out of the Congo.

When the outcry against the brutality of Leopold's agents persisted, in 1888 he ordered them to end some of their worst practices. No Congolese were to be forced to sign labor contracts, and all workers had to be guaranteed minimum wages. Local ombudsmen were designated to give fair hearings to all grievances. But at the same time, severe punishment was authorized for all Congolese who deserted a work force.

When Tippo-Tip was driven out of the Congo in 1890, the Arab slave trade revived. Tribes working for the Arabs attacked Belgian military posts and massacred the defenders. The slave traders also encouraged tribal warfare, enslaving the natives of defeated tribes. A new international conference at Brussels in July, 1890, gave Leopold the financial aid he asked for to crush the slavers. In clashes over the next 15 years, the Arabs lost 70,000 men.

The Berlin Act of 1885 had not defined the boundaries of the Congo Free State except to indicate that they would be defined by "effective occupation." In the southeastern corner of the Congo that was Katanga, the boundary line was crucial because the peripheral area was rich in mining ores.

"Effective occupation" by border posts and military camps required a treaty with M'Siri, chief of the powerful Bayeke, who controlled the perimeter from Bunkeya. Leopold learned that two of Rhodes's British agents had reached Bunkeya and were seeking to persuade M'Siri to sign a treaty with them.

The King had just concluded negotiations with Belgian financiers to form the Company of Katanga, with a 99-year concession to develop a third of all Katanga territory the company was able to annex. Four Belgian expeditions sped to the Congo to fan out through the region.

The first to reach Bunkeya was led by William Stairs, who found M'Siri to be a half-mad tyrant ruling with a 10,000-man army. In a palace of mud and thatch, surrounded by palisades crowned with the skulls of his enemies, the Bayeke chief indulged himself in unspeakable orgies of cruelty.

The Bayeke lived in terror and famine while M'Siri wallowed in wealth from trading in iron, ivory and slaves.

He refused Stairs's request for a treaty contemptuously. Speaking for Leopold, Stairs demanded M'Siri's abdication. On December 20, 1891, there was a furious altercation in which Stairs's aide, Captain Bodson, shot and killed M'Siri and was slain in turn. Stairs then negotiated a treaty with M'Siri's eldest son, Mukanda, who put Katanga under Leopold's rule in exchange for being allowed to remain Chief of the Bayeke.

To exploit his enlarged "slice of cake," Leopold granted industrial concessions to other large Belgian companies, including a railroad combine which was given mining rights in land opened up by their railway lines. Leopold's business partners soon exercised important influence over the administration of the Congo, especially in Katanga.

Gone were all pretenses of administering the Congo as a "noble trust for all civilization." The new business ventures applied strong pressure on colonial agents to show profits as quickly as possible. Leopold, holding a monopoly on Congo rubber, sought to fatten his fortune further by raising prices and slashing wages. Thousands of plantation workers, exercising the right he had guaranteed them, refused to sign labor contracts at starvation wages.

"From January 1, 1899, you must succeed in furnishing 4,000 kilos of rubber every month," Leopold ordered his agents. "To this effect I give you *carte blanche*. Employ gentleness at first, but if your people persist in not accepting the imposition of the State, employ force of arms."

The agents promptly organized night labor raids on sleeping villages by the Force Publique. These miserably paid troops were inducted from the most brutal, backward tribes, and were expected to live off what they seized from native villages. Congolese who fled or fought them were killed, and uncooperative villages were frequently burned.

The raids were often led by a Belgian agent carrying a lantern. Terrified blacks called him the *mundele ya mwinda* ("white man with a light"), whom many thought to be a powerful demon with a magic lantern that cast evil spells upon those it illuminated. His captives, set to work on a rubber plantation, were given a work quota. Those who failed to fill the quota were punished by having a hand or foot hacked off.

By 1903 the Congo Free State's exports of rubber were worth over $10 million, a fifth of it personal profit for Leopold. American and Swedish missionaries in the Congo were horrified by his slave labor system. They reported seeing baskets of severed hands from villagers punished for being too slow in delivering a rubber quota.

International indignation was aroused by a powerful novel by Joseph Conrad revealing what he had seen as a sea captain learning his trade on the Congo River. *Heart of Darkness* described chained Congolese forced to labor on the Congo railroad under armed overseers, and brutal white agents ordering "rebels" decapitated and their heads displayed on sticks to terrify other workers. "Pitiless, pitiless," one agent insisted, defending these practices. "That's the only way."

Edmund D. Morel, heading a Congo Reform Association, led a British crusade against Leopold's colonial rule, exposing it as a chamber of horrors. The British House of Commons, though no stranger to colonialism, was so shocked by Morel's collection of evidence that it decided unanimously in 1903 to consult with the other signatory powers of the Berlin Act on "measures . . . to abate the evils in that state."

On instructions from the British Parliament, Sir Roger Casement, British consul at Boma, submitted his own report in February, 1904. He told of seeing Congolese women and babies chained in sheds as hostages for the delivery of a village's rubber quota; Congolese beaten savagely at collection points for failure to bring in enough rubber; whole tribes fleeing their villages to escape mutilation; mass executions by white agents; and decapitated heads used as a decoration border around a flowerbed in an agent's yard.

Three million blacks, Casement estimated, had died through murder, mistreatment, starvation and disease during the 15 years of Leopold's exploitation of the Congo.

Such disclosures created a full-scale world uproar, spreading from Great Britain throughout Europe and the United States. Frightened, Leopold quickly organized a secret press bureau to propagandize journalists and editors on his behalf, and to bribe influential figures for public statements of support. But he was forced to agree to the dispatch of an independent international commission of inquiry.

His agents made sure that the three-man commission saw what Leopold wanted them to see, and were sheltered as much as possible from the unsavory aspects of his operations. After five months in the Congo the commission made its report:

"When one travels in the Congo and compares the older Congo, as we know it from the writings and descriptions of the explorers, with the Congo today, the impression received is one of admiration and wonder. The Free State, by the prodigies it has accomplished in twenty years, has given the world the . . . right to expect a great deal of it."

But they also admitted that there were indeed abuses of laborers in the Congo, and that reforms were obviously needed. Leopold hastily issued a series of new decrees for reforms based upon the commission's recommendations.

Time had run out on his credibility, however. In addition, there was a growing world climate of public indignation at the callous excesses of big business. Edmund D. Morel kept hammering home the contrast between the fat profits of Leopold and his partners and the misery of the Congo natives they exploited. A chief target was the Katanga Company, which in October, 1906, became Union Miniere. Its copper and other mineral exports gradually replaced rubber as the mainstay of the Congo economy.

In December, 1906, Henry Cabot Lodge, speaking for the Senate, urged President Theodore Roosevelt to demand an end to Leopold's one-man rule. Muckraking *Collier's* magazine sent Richard Harding Davis to the Congo in January, 1907.

Davis reported that he could not find a single school or hospital operated by the Belgians for the Congolese outside Boma, the Congo "showcase." He saw work performed by labor gangs linked by steel rings around their necks. In Leopoldville, waiting for a boat to take him upriver, he saw a drunken port officer order black soldiers to beat a crowd of native women seeking to cross to the French side of the Congo River. French traders paid mahogany cutters for a day's work what the Belgians paid as a monthly wage.

"Twenty million people are owned by one man," Davis wrote. "Even in the capital of Boma all the conditions of slavery exist. . . . In the jungle, away from the sight of men, all things are possible." Leopold, he reported, had cleared a personal profit of at least $25 million in the previous eight years from his private holdings and shares in business concessions.

"It is an incredible state of affairs," Davis reported. "so insolent, so magnificent in its impertinence, that it would be humorous were it not for its background of misery and sufferings, for its hostage houses, its chain gangs, its nameless crimes against the human body."

Mark Twain scathingly described Leopold as one of the "crowned beasts of Europe." American missionaries said that the United States, the first power to recognize Leopold's A.I.C. as the government of the Congo, had a moral obligation to end the atrocities. Many signatories of the Act of Berlin were anxious to get the Congo out of the world spotlight before questions were raised about their own African colonies.

Strong pressure was applied on the Brussels Parliament already deeply embarrassed by the uproar over Leopold's sordid African enterprise. After hot debate the Parliament forced him to relinquish control of the personal empire he had exploited for 23 years. On November 15, 1908, his Congo Free State ceased to exist, replaced by the Belgian Congo, a colony administered by the Belgian Government.

The new colonial administrators, appointed by Parliament, gave no representation to either white Belgians, most of them Leopold's agents, or black Congolese. All slave labor policies were abolished. A new program of primary and technical education began training Africans for industrial jobs. Proposals for advanced education for the brightest Congolese were rejected, however, on grounds that a fair system required "bringing all the people up together, equally."

The country was divided into six provinces—Leopoldville, Equator, Oriental, Kasai, Kivu and Katanga—each administered by a provincial governor under a governor-general representing Belgium. This arbitrary division of the Congo cut across tribal lines, perhaps in the belief that splitting up the tribes would make them easier to control. Congolese were allowed to be self-governing on the lowest level, operating their own village and tribal institutions.

Minimum-wage laws replaced forced labor. Decent homes began to be built for Congolese working in the mines and plantations. All employers were required to provide clothing and other necessities for their workers, as well as to serve them nutritious food. A system of missionary-operated medical care was organized that soon became the best in Africa.

The world furor over the Congo slowly subsided as it became apparent that the Belgians were indeed carrying out far-reaching reforms. The new policy, highly advanced for the colonialism of its day, was one of paternalism. The Governor-General behaved toward the Congolese like a father toward children, directing and controlling all their important affairs while looking after their welfare benevolently.

For the Congolese it was a wonderful change from the long nightmare they had endured under Leopold. But the fatal flaw of paternalism was eventually to have tragic consequences. When the Congolese were relegated to the dependent role of "the white man's burden," the Belgian Parliament felt no need to prepare them for a day when they would have to manage their own affairs as an independent nation.

The Colonial Charter of 1908 guaranteed many new civil liberties to all in the Congo—freedom of person, religion, job choice, opinion and education; inviolability of the home and mail; and rights of petition and legal action. To keep needed white specialists in the Congo, however, Brussels guaranteed separate privileges and courts for the white man in a country that belonged to the black man. The press was censored, and unauthorized meetings were forbidden "for reasons of public order"—i.e., to prevent the development of any black protest movement against white racism.

The whites in the Congo refused to concede that black Congolese, however intelligent or educated, could be their equals. They would not shake hands with an African, permit him in their bars or restaurants, tolerate him as a neighbor or invite him to their homes. In some communities curfew laws forbade blacks to leave the African quarter after dark.

Flogging was legal punishment for black men, but not for whites. All high-paying jobs went to the whites, all low-paying work to the blacks. Africans were kept from rising above the most minor posts in industry and administration.

Although the white settlers, like the blacks, had no formal voice in the colonial government, their influence was unmistakable. Brussels was cautious about encouraging large-scale white settlement in the Congo, however, fearing to aggravate racial tensions. Immigration was held down by compelling Belgians leaving for the Congo to post financial bonds guaranteeing that they would not become public charges.

Whites in the Congo looked upon it not as a homeland, as whites in Britain's African colonies did, but only as an outpost for building up a nest egg for retirement in Belgium. When the winds of independence began to blow strongly in the Congo, the whites simply resigned themselves to the prospect of "returning home" sooner. Since they, like the blacks, had never been given the right to vote in the Congo's affairs, they had never considered themselves anything but overseas Belgians.

Leopold II died in December, 1909, a year after Belgium's annexation of his fiefdom, and was succeeded by his nephew Albert I. Five years later, when the Kaiser invaded Belgium,

German troops in Africa also thrust into the eastern Congo. Congolese troops led by Belgian officers joined French and British forces in campaigns against the Germans in the Cameroons and Rhodesia, and helped capture German East Africa.

The Congo's biggest contribution to the Allied war effort, however, was its vast supply of vital copper. The wartime boom increased the number of firms operating in the Congo to 2,000. When World War I was over, Belgium's new Minister of the Colonies, Louis Franck, launched an ambitious new program of industrial expansion.

Ports were enlarged, airfields built, communications lengthened, new railroad lines begun. The economy was diversified by introducing large-scale stock-raising and by developing cotton, coffee and palm tree plantations. A mass educational system provided a black labor force with enough technical training to fill low-echelon jobs in the colony's booming industry and agriculture. But no native was educated beyond an eighth-grade level.

"We need them smart enough to do the work," one official admitted, "but not smart enough to kick us out!"

# 4
# A Black Middle Class
# Emerges

DURING WORLD WAR II, WHEN THE Germans again overran
Belgium, the Congo continued to be governed by the Belgian
Government from exile in London. The wealth of the Congo's
mines, plantations and forests was once more essential to the
sinews of the Allied war effort. With the loss of Southeast
Asia to the Japanese, Congo tin became vital to the Allies,
who also drew heavily on the colony's gold, cobalt, tungsten,
palm oil and rubber. But most important of all was uranium.

One day in 1942 an American colonel entered the New
York office of Union Miniere and asked the company's chairman, Edgar Sengier, if he could help the United States get
some uranium ore from the Congo in a hurry. He did not
dare tell Sengier the reason—production of a secret atom
bomb. But Sengier astonished him by declaring, "The ore is
here in New York, one thousand tons of it. I have been waiting for you." It was stored in steel drums in a New York
warehouse.

Sengier had been warned in Elizabethville by a British
physicist that the Germans were working on an atom bomb,
and might attack the Congo to get needed uranium. On his

own initiative he had shipped a thousand tons of it to New York, shrewdly surmising that the Americans would need it sooner or later. A grateful Washington later decorated him.

The economic boom stimulated by World War II brought a vast upsurge of white immigration to the Congo. The impact on the colony was so great that its relative isolation from the rest of the world ended. African workers grew increasingly resentful of a white prosperity in their own country that excluded them, and began to organize in unions.

Ninety were killed in bitter clashes at Union Miniere in 1942. There was further unrest in Kasai Province a year later when the Force Publique revolted because of low pay.

Hitler's defeat brought the Belgian Government back to Brussels on September 8, 1944. But there was a great deal of Belgian resentment of King Leopold III's quick surrender to Germany. It expressed itself in the election of many liberals and socialists to Parliament. Opposed to Belgium's colonial policies, they demanded a phasing out of paternalism and preparation of the Congolese for self-government.

Their pressure brought about the first high school in the Congo, soon followed by others. Young French-speaking graduates became a new Westernized elite known as "evolués." Recognized as Belgian citizens, they were rewarded with a special card entitling them to the privileges of citizenship.

Members of this tiny new black middle class were given jobs with the colonial administration as civil servants and teachers, and also became priests, white-collar workers and craftsmen.

Daily contact at work with Europeans made the evolués increasingly self-confident and ambitious. Forbidden to organize politically, they formed social, religious, labor and tribal clubs. Soon there were clandestine meetings of the clubs at which the evolués developed plans to win equal pay with whites, improved working conditions and opportunities, an end to racial discrimination and—the ultimate dream—independence for the Congo under black rule.

Evolué clubs of government clerks were the nuclei around which political parties later formed. In 1947 their pressure induced the Brussels Parliament to inaugurate a new program of Congolese social welfare. A $6 million annual budget began to provide hospitals, dispensaries, child care centers, orphan asylums, leprosauriums, community warehouses, fish-breeding centers and milk distribution depots.

Full employment also brought millions of Congolese a rising standard of living that was the highest of any African country. The boom was fueled even higher by American purchases of every ounce of uranium mined in the Congo at the end of the forties in a nuclear weapons race with the U.S.S.R.

But the evolués were far from satisfied. New hope and rising expectations made them impatient with the gradual pace of social reforms. One sore point was the Congo's penal code, which dispensed separate black and white justice.

In rural areas Government officials served as police court judges, with the power to jail any black who expressed a grievance against them as bureaucrats. White men, however, could be tried only in district courts which granted them all the European safeguards of a fair trial.

In 1947 the evolués were able to win the appointment of two Africans to each of the City Councils, which had previously been all-white. In Elizabethville, capital of Katanga and seat of Union Miniere's industrial empire, the first evolué so honored was Moise Kapenda ("Beloved Moses") Tshombe.

Related to Lunda tribal royalty, Tshombe was born in 1919 at Masumba, tribal capital of Katanga. He was the eldest of six sons of the first Congolese to be worth a million francs through ownership of plantations, retail stores, a fleet of trucks, a hotel and a sawmill. Educated at an American Methodist mission and trained as a teacher and accountant, young Tshombe was entrusted with management of his father's businesses in Elizabethville.

A pudgy, large-eyed country youth, he was dazzled by the change from the remote bush country of his school days to the modern avenues and glittering nightclubs of Katanga's capital. Neglecting the family enterprises, he caroused around the city in a flashy car. His angry father recalled him, presented him with a string of rural stores and told Moise to sink or swim with them.

The young playboy went bankrupt three times, and had to be rescued twice by his despairing father when he was arrested for passing worthless checks.

He was more successful in a marital venture, however, winning for his wife the favorite daughter of the chief of the powerful Lunda tribe. Through her connections and his father's, Tshombe won the appointment to the Elizabethville City Council. He quickly showed shrewd talent for pragmatic politics, and was made President of the Elizabethville African Chamber of Commerce.

At the beginning of his career Tshombe was not particularly pro-Belgian, only pro-Tshombe. Without scruples or principles, he was a corrupt opportunist who directed his career flexibly along the channels of power, wherever they lay at any particular moment. A chuckling, personable, enigmatic figure, he was to demonstrate a ruthless talent for survival in the political jungle. It was Tshombe whose cunning maneuvers would later plunge the Congo into civil war and force the United Nations into crisis.

Another evolué emerged into the spotlight in 1950 when Joseph Kasavubu formed a "cultural association" in Leopoldville known as ABAKO, representing the Bakongo. A short, squat, bespectacled African who admired Mahatma Gandhi, Kasavubu was a cautious man of infinite patience. Sooner or later, he was convinced, black leadership of the Congo would fall into his lap like a ripe plum.

Born near the Atlantic at Tshela, Leopoldville Province, in 1917, he entered a seminary after graduating secondary school to study for the priesthood. An unsuccessful candidate, he left three years later to teach, then became a Government supply clerk in Leopoldville.

Joining a study group that later evolved into ABAKO, he rose to prominence with a speech called "The Right of the First Occupant." The Congo, Kasavubu insisted, belonged to those who had occupied it first— the Bakongo, to whom Belgium ought to return it. To strengthen tribal loyalties, he sought to revive the ancient Bakongo language as a common bond, just as Irish revolutionaries had tried to unite Irishmen against the English by reviving Gaelic.

Kasavubu, like most evolués, had ambivalent feelings about the paternalism of the Belgians. On one hand, the evolués' own education and advancement was in itself a tribute to postwar Belgian liberalism, especially in contrast to the harsh, repressive treatment of Africans in other countries.

But paternalism was fatally flawed by racism. Although their citizenship cards presumably put evolués on an equal basis with whites, the Belgians in the Congo refused to accept them as social equals. Even the missionaries who operated Congolese schools and hospitals did not hesitate to indicate feelings of racial superiority.

The average European in the Congo derisively referred to Africans, however well educated, as *"macaques* (monkeys) only recently down from the trees." Such cruel slurs stung the evolués, making them grimly determined to attain a power status that would force the whites to respect African dignity. It did not help matters that before white officials awarded an evolué a citizenship card, he had to prove to them that his education and way of life made him "civilized enough."

"I wanted to assure them that I would never do the barbaric things King Leopold II had done," said one embittered evolué who knew his Congo history, "but in a white colony one learns to bite a black tongue."

In 1951 evolué pressure, largely from Kasavubu's ABAKO, persuaded Belgium to add eight African members to the governor-general's advisory council. The Brussels Parliament also passed a new billion-dollar Ten-Year Plan in 1952 to accelerate programs of public health, hygiene, education and housing. A medical campaign began wiping out such old scourges of the Congo as malaria and sleeping sickness.

But despite such willingness to conciliate the evolués, Belgium saw no need to give them any share of real power.

"There was until recently hardly any real thought of transferring effective responsibility from European to African shoulders," wrote one observer, George Carpenter, in 1953. "It was believed that the present pattern of relationships might continue more or less unchanged for a century or more."

49

The American viewpoint that year was expressed by the State Department's Chester Bowles: "The danger lies not so much in the possibility that the Belgians will not compromise eventually with the force of nationalism, but that when they do they will find the Africans almost totally inexperienced in handling the responsibilities which they are certain to demand and eventually to get."

It was a remarkably shrewd prophecy.

The evolués bitterly resented the segregation policies in Congo schools. Colonial authorities insisted that separate facilities were necessary because African children had to be taught in tribal tongues, with regard for local customs. This, they alleged, was why white education could proceed at a faster pace and to a higher level.

They pointed to the large growth of schools as proof of their sincere effort on behalf of mass education for the Congolese. But the evolués were not impressed. They knew that most Congolese still did not get beyond a second-grade level, and many lapsed back into illiteracy afterwards.

Few reached high school. Even in the year the Congo became independent, the educational system produced only 136 African high school graduates. A bare handful of evolués were permitted to go abroad to attend a European university, and then usually only in Brussels. The first was Thomas Kanza, who later became the Congo's first minister to the U.N.

The Belgian colonial office dreaded the example of European-educated Jomo Kenyatta, who had returned to Kenya after World War II to lead a militant nationalist movement against English colonialism, provoking Mau Mau uprisings.

"We have seen that those natives who have been shown Europe and given an advanced education," declared the Belgian Colonial Minister in April, 1954, "do not always return with a spirit favorable to civilization and to the mother country in particular." To keep ambitious evolués at home, a native college, Lovanium University, was opened at Kisanti.

As black nationalist movements swept through other African countries, Brussels grew increasingly worried about the Congo. On May 16, 1955, King Baudoin paid a visit to Leopoldville to strengthen black support for the Crown. Encouraged by a crowd of over 200,000 Congolese who turned out to hear him, he made a tour of the Congo. He was hailed everywhere as the great white chief who had improved the quality of daily life for the average Congolese. Baudoin was delighted.

"The time will come," he promised a meeting of the postal workers' "Friendly Society" in Stanleyville (Oriental Province), "which will assure to each, white or black, his proper share in the country's government, according to his own qualities and capacity. Before we realize this high ideal, gentlemen, much remains to be done."

In a private meeting the King discussed evolué complaints at some length with an impressive young African in thick-lensed glasses, Patrice Lumumba, who had organized the postal workers of the Congo and was their spokesman.

Lumumba had been born in the mudhut village of Katako Kombe (Kasai Province) in 1925. His parents were devout Catholic members of the small, warlike Batetela tribe. Sent to a mission school, he was expelled for fighting with his teachers, who found him a brilliant student but moody and unpredictable. Over his parents' protest, he abandoned Catholicism and transferred to a Protestant mission school.

His smouldering nature did not permit him to remain in

school beyond the eighth grade. Employed as a servant by a Protestant missionary, the trigger-tempered Lumumba stole his employer's watch and enough money for the fare to Stanleyville. There he applied for a job as a postal clerk. Asked for a character reference, Lumumba coolly applied for one from the missionary he had robbed. The kindly pastor gave it to him.

As a postal clerk Lumumba continued to educate himself through correspondence courses in French law, literature, philosophy, economics, social sciences and administration. He received sympathetic help in these studies from European teachers in Stanleyville who admired his brilliance.

Like other evolués, Lumumba had been drawn into the anticolonial movement. Impatient, impulsive and inexperienced, he was nevertheless a persuasive orator and a magnetic leader. Unlike Tshombe, whose sole interest lay in Katanga, or Kasavubu, who wanted a restoration of Bakongo power, Lumumba saw the future of the Congo as a black republic unifying all tribes and provinces. It was this vision which was to lift him above all other evolué leaders in the struggle for change.

That struggle received powerful impetus in December, 1955, with publication of a book by a Belgian professor, A. J. J. van Bilsen, *A Thirty-Year Plan for the Political Emancipation of Belgian Africa.* Van Bilsen, a lawyer who taught at the Antwerp University Institute for Overseas Territories, had traveled extensively in the Congo, and was appalled by Belgium's failure to prepare Congolese to take over their own affairs.

"It is our fault, not theirs, that there are no doctors, veterinarians, engineers, functionaries or officers among them," he said. Colonial authorities made grudging concessions to the Congolese only when they had to, he noted, and barred the upper levels of responsibility to Africans.

Warning that the failure to plan for a Congolese-run Congo would bring on rebellion and chaos, Van Bilsen urged Belgium to help the evolués develop "a grand Congolese federation" of provinces under African control.

"The colonial imperialism of the past half century," he admonished, "is gone forever." Belgian conservatives were outraged by his attack, but liberals and socialists hailed it as farsighted and long overdue. Its greatest impact, however, was upon the evolués themselves.

Van Bilsen's bombshell emboldened them to begin speaking out openly for independence. Social clubs revealed themselves in their true colors as political parties. Different factions began to clash in a contest for leadership of a future republic of the Congo, which suddenly, in 1956, had been transformed from dream to possibility.

*Conscience Africain*, a magazine published by the Bangala tribe, ran a special manifesto in July inspired by the Van Bilsen 30-year plan of gradual independence. It was written by the editor, Joseph Ileo, an evolué moderate with a reputation for originality and wisdom. Born in Leopoldville in 1922, Ileo had studied philosophy and sociology in high school. He saw the Van Bilsen plan as a way to win racial equality for Africans without destroying their own unique culture.

"We wish to be civilized Congolese, not dark-skinned Europeans," Ileo declared. "We understand well that the Europeans wish to maintain their own way of life (but) we reject with vehemence the principle of 'equal but separate.'" He demanded full political participation for Africans in Congo affairs, leading eventually to self-government.

"Belgium must not consider that there is a feeling of hostility in our desire for emancipation. Quite to the contrary, Belgium should be proud that, unlike nearly all colonized people, our desire is expressed without hatred or resentment. This alone is undeniable proof that the work of the Belgians in this country is not a failure."

He was not suggesting, Ileo explained, that the Belgians should abandon the Congo, but only their racism, political domination and economic exploitation. He wanted them to stay in the Congo and cooperate with Africans as equal partners. But if they failed to develop the evolués as responsible leaders, he warned, they could only expect to encourage demagogues to inflame the country into a black revolution.

Opposing the creation of African political parties, Ileo feared that these would only divide the Congolese against themselves. He wanted the evolués to unite in a National Popular Movement, with *Conscience Africain* as its spokesman. To assure colonial authorities that he was only asking for self-government under the Belgian flag, Ileo concluded: "We cry out: Long live the Congo! Long live Belgium! Long live the King!"

His manifesto had an electrifying effect throughout the Congo. Copies of that issue of *Conference Africain* were passed from hand to hand until they fell apart. Read aloud to illiterates, the manifesto was also translated into dozens of tribal tongues. What astonished the Congolese was not only the Bangala tribe's bold demands, but that they dared to make any demands at all.

Belgians braced anxiously for the approaching storm.

54

# 5
# The Winds of Change

KASAVUBU WAS CHAGRINED BY ILEO'S success in putting the
Bangala in the vanguard of the emancipation movement. He
counterattacked in a speech in August, 1956, making it clear
that the Bakongo of ABAKO rejected Ileo's plea for a single
African movement in order to avoid political struggle.

"It is purely utopian to try to rally all the Congolese to
the same opinion," Kasavubu insisted. "The struggles of
parties, although dangerous, is very necessary in a democracy." He also demanded an end to rule of the Congo from
Belgium. "None of us were at the Berlin Conference," he
cried. "And yet everything was decided for us there!"

He rejected Van Bilsen's 30-year plan: "In reality it is
only the same old lullaby. Our patience is already exhausted.
Since the hour has come, emancipation should be granted us
this very day rather than delayed for another 30 years!"
Otherwise, he warned grimly, it would arrive in the Congo
through "hatred, revolt, separation."

Kasavubu called for a Congolese Federation of tribes with
a Parliament of democratically elected representatives, and
for a full Bill of Rights for Africans. He scorned Van Bilsen's

proposal to give the Congo the status of a Belgian province. "Is it possible," he asked "to conceive how this Congo, 80 times larger than Belgium, could become its 'tenth province'?" He called instead for ties between them to be shaped along the lines of the British Commonwealth.

African outcries from what had once been described as "an empire of silence" were heard across the Atlantic. Washington grew concerned that the situation might turn revolutionary, giving the Soviet Union a chance to gain a foothold in central Africa. Through the U.N. the United States sought to apply pressure on Belgium to conciliate the evolués.

Brussels journalists charged Washington with seeking to pose as the world champion of underdeveloped countries. They insisted that "premature autonomy" for a colonial people unprepared to handle it could end in an anarchy far more dangerous than any possible turn toward Communism.

The Belgian Government testily accused the U.N. of meddling in its internal affairs, but sent a special commission to the Congo to confer with leading evolués on their demands and views. The evolués were made suspicious, however, by the sudden arrest on July 1, 1956, of silver-tongued Patrice Lumumba, now President of the Stanleyville Evolués Circle, for embezzling $2,200 from money orders in his job at the post office. Was the Government trying to stigmatize and discredit the trustworthiness of evolué leadership?

But Belgian administrators had noticed that Lumumba not only owned a car, unusual for a postal clerk, but also lived far beyond his means. An audit of the books revealed the shortage in his accounts. At first he insisted that the money had been taken to further the cause of black nationalism.

Sentenced to two years in prison, he appealed, claiming he had taken the blame for a crime of his subordinates.

When his loyal followers promised to raise and restore the amount of the missing funds, his sentence was reduced to one year. The tall, bearded prisoner received a cheering reception when he returned to Stanleyville in 1957.

The evolués told the Belgian commission that only a self-governing Congo could end the glaring inequity in the treatment of blacks and whites. Despite all of Brussels' welfare programs for blacks, 13 million Congolese were now paid only $42 a year in cash per capita, in contrast to an average of $2,800 annually for 115,000 whites in the colony.

Aware that the winds of change blowing in the Congo would soon become a gale, Union Miniere enlisted a prominent African auxiliary who could be trusted to protect the company's huge investments in Katanga. Their choice was the incorrigible playboy Moise Tshombe, whose sophisticated gaiety, charm and flamboyance made him a favorite with Europeans.

Operating through the Governor of Katanga, Union Miniere financed Tshombe in building a power base opposed to the evolués who were demanding a centralized black Congo republic. Exercising his prestige as son-in-law of the chief of the Lunda, Tshombe founded the Lunda Tribal Association in 1956. "Katanga for the Katangais!" he shrilled.

The governor-general, meanwhile, grew increasingly worried by spreading black unrest, fanned by Ileo and Kasavubu. In August, 1957, to "safeguard public order," a weekly called *Congo* was seized and banned for calling for emancipation.

"The paper was banned because the truths of colonial reality are not to be published and divulged," charged Thomas

Kanza, the Congo's first university graduate. "They are simply to be borne with joys and smiles. . . . This suppression was a grave political error for the Belgians!"

The colonial government was especially sensitive to nationalist agitation at this time because a world recession had caused a sharp price slump for Congo exports, and the economy was hard hit. Unless Brussels came to the colony's assistance with huge loans, many projects under development would have to be halted. Millions of Congolese would be thrown out of work, and welfare programs halted.

Consulting with his white advisory council, the governor-general decided it might be prudent to begin yielding some black power on the municipal level, where evolués could be useful both as targets for discontent and in controlling any riots sparked by unemployment or black nationalism.

Voting districts of the cities and environs were divided into unequal white and black zones, to ensure white domination of the new municipal councils. For the first time black and white Congolese went to the polls to elect local officials of their own choice. Evolués were jubilant at having forced the authorities to introduce democracy into the Congo and to recognize their right to enter local politics.

There was an immediate and confusing proliferation of political parties growing out of the social clubs and tribal associations. But it quickly became clear that parties and platforms meant little to the unsophisticated Congolese. They cheered candidates on a basis of personality and tribal ties, and how well they castigated the whites in their speeches.

In the struggle to become the first elected officials of the Congo, ambitious evolués often switched sides with bewildering frequency. Yesterday's allies would become today's enemies; today's enemies would become tomorrow's allies. For most the driving force was not principle but personal power. That pattern would persist, confusing the world, except for black citizens of other countries, who knew the desperation of being locked, powerless, into a ghetto.

The election quickly assumed tribal overtones. In Leopoldville there were clashes between Kasavubu's Bakongo and Ileo's Bangala. Both factions were about equal in strength, but the popular and powerful Kasavubu was also a master organizer. His appearances for ABAKO in a leopard skin, symbolizing ancient Bakongo power, drew immense crowds.

He called publicly for a free Congo republic. But his admirers knew that "King Kasa" really wanted a restoration of the old great Kingdom of the Bakongo. There was little doubt about what tribe would rule the roost if he had his way.

In Katanga Province, Tshombe campaigned on a platform of close cooperation with the Belgians, stressing the paternal advantages to his Lunda. He was fiercely opposed by Jason Sendwe, whose bright Baluba tribesmen straddled both Katanga and Kasai. Sendwe had been educated by Methodist mission schools in north Katanga as a medical assistant, minister and teacher. Appointed consultant to the colonial administration in 1942, he was respected by both races for his ability to speak 14 languages and for a book on Baluba culture.

Sendwe attacked Tshombe for urging a regionalism that would leave Katanga under the thumb of Union Miniere.

The municipal elections of December, 1957, polarized Congolese around the issue of nationalism versus regionalism. Sendwe accepted an invitation to join Lumumba and Ileo to work for immediate independence and a strong Congo republic. Their "study group" was joined by Cyrille Adoula, representing the Belgian General Confederation of Labor.

Kasavubu stood aloof from the nationalist movement, determined upon either Bakongo supremacy or separation.

The popular Lumumba's prison record did not interfere with his appointment as commercial director of a Leopoldville beer company, a post in which he rapidly prospered. Speaking for independence in tweed suits and bow ties, he impressed the large crowds he attracted by his spellbinding eloquence. He was careful, however, not to incur new Belgian wrath.

He credited Belgium with having eradicated disease, ended barbaric tribal practices and developed the Congolese into "free, happy, vigorous, civilized men." He also reminded his countrymen: "To whom do we owe our liberation from that odious trade practiced by the bloodthirsty Arabs and their allies, those inhuman brigands who ravaged our country?"

But, at the same time, he appealed directly to the Belgian conscience: "Do not destroy the African's soul by attempting to make the African a superficial caricature of a European, a black-skinned Westerner. . . . Your principles and ideas may be good for you, but they do not suit the Africans." He urged Belgian acceptance of M.N.C.'s goal of a black Congo republic, insisting they would not suffer by it.

"If the Congo should obtain its independence tomorrow, why should you leave us, and why should we drive you out, so long as our coexistence gives rise to no friction and so long as we continue to treat each other as true friends?"

Lumumba shrewdly sought to set himself apart from other evolué leaders by proclaiming his identity with the African masses. Knowing that most Congolese admired the evolués but resented their airs of superiority and their privileges, he subtly reproached fellow evolués for arrogance.

"Let us not stand aloof from our brothers," he exhorted piously, "because they are less educated, less cultured, less fortunate than ourselves. . . . We want to bridge the gulf which separates us from the whites, but we must not create another one behind us. Who will work for them if we abandon them? May they not one day turn against us?"

Women's support was solicited by another thrust at his rivals: "Can we honestly claim to be evolués when we leave our wives and children to eat on the ground like savages whilst we ourselves eat at table?"

The governor-general, hoping to blunt the drive for emancipation by persuading Congolese that the municipal elections marked a turning-point in black-white relations, decreed that after December, 1957, any act of racial prejudice or hostility would be considered a criminal offense punishable by up to a year in jail and a 3,000-franc fine. Most Congo Belgians shrugged off the decree as a political gesture that might be enforced against blacks but never against them.

The principal victors in the municipal elections were not advocates of a black republic but evolués who emphasized sectional tribal power. Kasavubu and ABAKO triumphed in Leopoldville over Ileo in a sizable victory that made him Mayor of Dendale, one of the city's important black communes. In Katanga, Tshombe's CONAKAT easily defeated Jason Sendwe, who was no match for his opponent in demagoguery or charisma.

But the elections failed to extinguish Lumumba's spark of nationalist agitation. It caught fire in 1958, a turning-point in Congolese history, from the winds of change blowing from other African countries revolting against colonialism.

The first large new flame crackled on April 20, 1958, when the usually cautious Kasavubu shocked the colonial establishment by his inaugural speech as Mayor of Dendale.

In an unexpected attack on the administration, Kasavubu demanded an end to press censorship; college education for blacks; promotion of black troops and police to officer rank; and national elections to change the Congo from a white colony to a black democracy. The stunned governor-general had barely recovered when he was handed another blow from General Charles de Gaulle himself, on a visit to Brazzaville, across the river from Leopoldville.

On August 24, De Gaulle told the French Congolese, "Whoever wishes independence can have it as soon as he wishes." He offered them a choice, by ballot, between independence and autonomous membership within a French community. Congolese evolués in Leopoldville were stunned by the magnanimity of the French. Why didn't the Belgians make the same offer?

The worried colonial minister hastily reminded the world of Belgium's contributions to the Congo: "When we came to Africa the natives had to be taught everything. They knew nothing of writing or building. They had no idea of what a nation was, or a state or even a slightly developed political organization." *Inforcongo*, the Belgian propaganda agency, emphasized Brussel's fatherly care of the Congolese, providing their food, clothes, education and medicine.

But it was precisely this paternalism, denying them the dignity of adult responsibility, that the evolués now most sorely resented. And in practice even the best-educated, most polite and intelligent evolués were not accepted by white Belgians as equals, despite the citizenship cards.

"We must be honest about it," said a Union Miniere official defensively in private. "Even the evolués are still savages in business suits. We must remember that they were all up in trees just 50 years ago. We cannot expect to make Europeans out of them overnight. It will take centuries."

The governor-general's law against racial discrimination had obviously done nothing to alter white prejudice.

But De Gaulle's offer to liberate the French Congo had made it impossible for Brussels to maintain the status quo in the Belgian Congo. Two days afterward a petition asking for independence, signed by all of Leopoldville's evolués, was presented to the Minister of the Belgian Congo, M. Petillon.

The upset Belgian Government reacted with a swift series of moves designed to appease the evolués. The first African family was speedily moved into the white section of Leopoldville. Government officials made vigorous statements denouncing racial prejudice. Colonial officials were ordered to begin cultivating evolué leaders socially at once.

That summer and fall, Brussels held an International Exposition. The Belgian Government flew in several hundred evolués to staff seven pavilions showing achievements in the Congo. Other evolués were brought to Brussels as guests.

The impact on the Africans was more profound than the Belgians had expected, and in different ways. The evolués were excited by what amounted to the first opportunity to gather from all over the Congo in what became an informal convention. The exposition also gave them a picture of the whole Congo and its operations that they found tremendously educational. Many began thinking on national rather than regional levels.

Some were astonished to discover that the Belgians they met in Brussels, along with whites from all over the world, behaved far more democratically than the Belgian colonists. They felt a new dignity in being treated as mature men instead of being patronized as primitive children.

They were especially fascinated by observing white behavior in the exposition's amusement center, *La Belgique Joyeuse.* "Many colonial tourists," Thomas Kanza noted of his fellow evolués, "learned that man is everywhere the same, that human qualities as well as virtues and faults are not the monopoly of any people."

On October 10, 1958, Joseph Ileo, whose *Conscience Africain* manifesto had first sounded the tocsin for self-government, organized the evolués who had signed the petition for independence into a new political party, the National Congolese Movement( M.N.C.). Joining the M.N.C. were such important leaders as Patrice Lumumba, Cyrille Adoula, Albert Kalonji and Joseph Mobutu.

Lumumba was chosen to prepare a press release on M.N.C. To the consternation of his fellow members, he brazenly listed himself as president. But they decided to let his maneuver go unchallenged rather than precipitate an internal struggle before the infant organization had even taken its first feeble steps. Hostility toward him intensified, however, as he began making fiery speeches for M.N.C. which other members objected to as far too militant and provocative.

Concern was also felt by the white colonists, especially in Katanga. The province had a third of the Congo's white population, including 3,000 officials. A strong, independent

Congo Government, with centralized black control in Leopold-ville, would have Union Miniere at its mercy.

Tshombe's Lunda were equally opposed to federalism. They were largely satisfied with Union Miniere's paternalism, which provided workers with homes, schools and even, in 1956, a state university at Elizabethville, one of two in the whole country. They also resented the federalist-minded Baluba for competing successfully with them for Union Miniere jobs.

The job stakes were high. Over half the people in Katanga, black as well as white, drew salaries from some phase of Union Miniere's vast mining operations. Katanga provided a third of everything consumed domestically in the Congo, half of its exports and two-fifths of its revenue.

To strengthen Tshombe's hand against M.N.C., in October, 1958, Union Miniere supplied him with funds to organize CONAKAT, a confederation of the Lunda, Bayeke and 16 smaller tribes into what amounted to a revival of the old Lunda Kingdom. Tshombe appointed as his lieutenant Gode-froid Munongo, grandson of M'Siri, who now led the Beyeke in Katanga.

CONAKAT stood for tribal interests supported by close ties to Belgium. Union Miniere would not need to fear any threat to its industrial empire as long as Moise Tshombe ruled over an autonomous Katanga Province. White colonists also saw CONAKAT as a valuable tool for sharpening tribal rival-ries and splitting the movement for black nationalism.

Jason Sendwe countered Tshombe's move by organizing his Baluba into a tribal party called BALUBAKAT. His party newpaper published a list of 50 prominent white colo-nists it promised to drive out of the Congo 24 hours after independence.

Brussels sped still another all-white commission to the Congo to investigate the rapidly changing political situation and make recommendations. It found, ironically, that the only one of the Congo's seven cities that had a black majority on its City Council was Elizabethville in Katanga.

"Why not?" laughed an M.N.C. official derisively. "Black puppets look better on white strings!"

In December, 1958, Kwame Nkrumah, Prime Minister of Ghana, newly freed by the British, held an All-African Peoples' Conference in Accra to coordinate the struggle for independence among African colonies. Lumumba attended and was greatly impressed by Nkrumah's accomplishment in creating a viable republic out of a colony with many deep tribal divisions.

Addressing the Ghana Conference on December 11, Lumumba attacked Belgian "injustices and abuses," and cited the U.N. Charter's Universal Declaration of Human Rights as justification for M.N.C.'s struggle for liberation. Condemning Tshombe's call for provincial autonomy, he cried, "Down with colonization and imperialism! Down with racism and tribalism!"

He returned to the Congo with Nkrumah's encouragement ringing in his ears, determined to force a showdown with Belgian colonialism. On December 28, before a crowd of 7,000 in the Leopoldville commune of Kalamu, he delivered a fiery speech that touched off the first violence.

# 6
# "I Am the Congo!"

HE CALLED FOR IMMEDIATE INDEPENDENCE, with "the masses and the elite to take control of public affairs." Demanding, not asking, Lumumba cried: "It is a *right* that the Congolese people have lost!" The crowd roared approval.

They were in an ugly mood. An influx of rural Congolese from the bush in search of urban prosperity had made 25,000 Congolese jobless in Leopoldville. Surging from the meeting, idlers began shouting imprecations at Europeans driving by; some threw stones. Others broke into shops and looted.

Not to be outdone, on January 4, 1959, Kasavubu called a mass meeting of his own in Kalamu. Reporting rejection of his demands for Bakongo autonomy by Belgium, he worked up the 4,000 Bakongo listening to him to such a fury that worried Leopoldville authorities called in police squads. Their appearance inflamed the Bakongo even more. Clashes with the police turned into a full-scale riot.

The crowd rampaged through Leopoldville, smashing property, destroying mission schools and attacking Europeans on the street. Martial law was declared. Force Publique troops were rushed in, reinforced by volunteer platoons of armed

European civilians. Street battles raged for three days. Troops and police employed armored cars and mortar units, firing on any Africans spotted on the street after dark.

Before order was restored on January 7, 49 Congolese had been killed, and 241 blacks and 49 whites wounded. ABAKO was banned. Kasavubu and his top aides were arrested and exiled to Belgium. Stunned Belgians demanded a quick compromise with evolué demands. Some Parliamentarians felt that Belgium should wash its hands of the Congo and its troubles as quickly as possible, accepting independence as inevitable.

Others argued that a pullout would only plunge the Congo into total chaos. Still others agreed, but favored that development to prove to Belgians, Congolese and the world the necessity for Belgium's continued colonial presence.

A Belgian study group in the Congo was ordered to rush its report. On January 8, 1959, it revealed its conclusions. The fruits of paternalism in the Congo had been Government bureaucracy, white racism, unemployment, overcrowded cities, a school shortage, press censorship and racial discrimination in the police and Force Publique.

Contributing to native unrest, the study group explained, were tribal rivalries, as well as the agitating influence of such pan-Africanism as Nkrumah's Accra Conference.

On January 13 the Belgian Government announced a new program for the evolution of self-government in the Congo:

"Belgium intends to organize in the Congo a democracy capable of exercising its prerogatives of sovereignty and of deciding on its independence."

The historic declaration swept through the Congo on a tidal

wave of native exultation. Patrice Lumumba hailed it as a great fulfillment of African hopes.

But the Bakongo, whose bloodshed had brought about this abrupt change of Belgian policy, were far from appeased. Their party, ABAKO, was still banned. Their leader, Kasavubu, was still in exile with his aides. So the Bakongo launched a campaign of passive resistance against the colonial government.

Ignoring all regulations, they set up their own tribal administration, awarding themselves autonomy. Colonial officials in Leopoldville, fearing to provoke open warfare with the Bakongo, simply ignored their disobedience.

Lumumba demanded a specific date for independence.

"I have no right to sleep," he told enthusiastic crowds, "as long as the people are not masters of their own destiny!" Seeking to establish himself as the father of his country, he cried, "I am the Congo! The Congo has made me—I am making the Congo!" His lack of identification with any powerful tribe or religious sect helped his image as an evolué dedicated to the ideal of a black, unified Congo, serving all tribes and sects without favoritism.

On April 12, 1959, he called a private meeting of eight political parties in Luluabourg (Kasai Province), and persuaded them to join with M.N.C. in demanding an independent republic by January, 1961. It was the first national political meeting ever held in the Congo.

Lumumba then flew to Brussels to urge the exiled Kasavubu to join his coalition. Asked to deliver a university lecture on the situation in the Congo, he flattered Kasavubu as the Congo patriot "who has had the courage to start the struggle against colonialism." But Kasavubu held aloof.

Returning home, Lumumba found the governor-general escorting the Belgian colonial minister on a tour of the Congo. Lumumba snapped some orders, and the officials were confronted wherever they went by demonstrations with hostile signs:

NO MORE COLONIAL MINISTERS; NO MORE GOVERNOR GENERALS!
THE YEAR '59: LAST COLONIAL GOVERNMENT
INDEPENDENCE OR DEATH!

In May, 1959, the Belgian Government let Kasavubu return to the Congo. ABAKO promptly revived under his leadership.

The civil disobedience campaign of the Bakongo now frequently became open defiance of the Government. Ignoring Lumumba's appeal for national unity, "King Kasa" prepared to break away the lower Congo as a Bakongo realm free of ties.

On June 24, Lumumba led leaders of his coalition of eight political parties to a conference with Minister of the Congo Van Hemelrijck. Presenting their timetable for independence, he demanded communal and territorial elections by December; provincial elections by March, 1960; and national elections by June, resulting in a parliament and new government.

But on that same day Kasavubu sent Van Hemelrijck an ultimatum of his own. ABAKO demanded that on January, 1960, the Province of Leopoldville become the autonomous Republic of Central Kongo. The "K" for Kongo emphasized his intention of making this region the private domain of the Bakongo tribe.

Van Hemelrijck coldly informed Kasavubu that Belgium would never allow Leopoldville Province to be split away from the Congo. Kasavubu countered with the proposal that it be given autonomy as part of a federated Congo. Van Hemelrijck rejected this plan, too, as "Balkanizing" the Congo into an unstable crazy quilt of small tribal nations. He warned both Kasavubu and Lumumba against rash moves.

"Law and order must be maintained," he insisted. "Troublemakers, whoever they are, must be brought to their senses. The time has come for firmness. We shall permit no departure from the Government Declaration."

On July 1, Lumumba counterattacked at an M.N.C. general assembly. Accusing Belgium of delaying independence in the hope of setting up a fraudulent republic in which black puppets would be manipulated by white colonists, he shouted, "Down with colonialism! Down with the Belgo-Congolese community! Down with the politics of intimidation! Down with the saboteurs of the Congo! Long live immediate independence!"

Lumumba's militancy began to frighten other M.N.C. leaders, notably Joseph Ileo, the party's philosophical founder. His objections to Lumumba's fiery speeches brought about a schism within M.N.C. The moderate faction fell away from Lumumba, following Ileo's leadership. On July 16, Ileo demanded that Lumumba resign as "dictator" of M.N.C. But Lumumba, knowing his 450,000 followers in M.N.C. were a majority, refused.

Ileo and Cyrille Adoula led an exodus of their supporters into the Kasai branch of M.N.C., headed by Albert Kalonji, also a moderate. Their faction became known as "M.N.C.-Kalonji." Lumumba was infuriated by this desertion. Without Ileo and Kalonji his claim that M.N.C. was the only Congolese political party with national support, therefore the only one that could form a stable republic, was no longer valid.

The M.N.C. split strengthened the hand of Moise Tshombe in Katanga, His CONAKAT Party, now openly subsidized by nion Miniere, called for "Katanga for the Katangais."

The Congo cauldron seethed further when tribal war threatened to break out between the Baluba and Bena Lulua tribes in Luluabourg. Kasai Province had once been the traditional home of the Bena Lulua, who had originally enslaved the nomadic Baluba when they had first moved into the region. But under Belgian rule the Baluba, a highly intelligent tribe, had risen above the Bena Lulua as merchants and local officials.

The resentful chief of the Bena Lulua now demanded that the Belgians turn Kasai over to him as an independent kingdom. The Baluba were frightened when the Kasai governor indicated support for this plan. It would mean, they knew, their extermination. Albert Kalonji, speaking for M.N.C.-Kalonji at a public meeting in Luluabourg on August 3, accused the colonial administration of favoring regionalism in order to keep Katanga safe for Union Miniere under Tshombe.

When violence broke out between the Bena Lulua and the Baluba, Kalonji and two aides were arrested on charges of inciting racial hatred. Despite Kalonji's defection, and perhaps hoping to win him back, Lumumba flew to Brussels to demand his release from the Colonial Minister. Sentenced to three months in jail, Kalonji was freed earlier in the hope of restoring some calm to Kasai.

The sudden outbreak of rioting there was only a prelude to more terrible tribal clashes to come, waiting only for the Belgian lid to lift off ancient hatreds in the Congo.

Meanwhile, in Belgium itself, pressure was building up for granting the Congolese independence as swiftly as possible. The colony was virtually bankrupt because of the depressed export market, and in 1959 drained $54 million in aid from Brussels. Many Belgians begrudged the expenditure as a subsidy to Union Miniere and other big Belgian corporations.

On October 16, a new minister of the Belgian Congo, Auguste de Schrijver, announced a timetable for independence. Local elections would be held in December for all seats on city and territorial councils. Soon afterward province councils would be formed, made up of elected Congolese (90 per cent) and Brussels appointees (10 per cent).

By the end of 1960 a new Central Government, with African representatives, would preside over a gradual evolution into independence, to be complete in 1964. The plan was a realistic one. Four years was little enough time to train evolués in the complexities of running their own country. There was still not a single African in any senior post of the civil administration, armed forces, communications and medical and transport services.

To Lumumba, however, the Belgian plan was only a scheme to bribe the evolués with local power, while perpetuating colonial control of the national structure. Local elections, he feared, would only serve to polarize tribal rivalries and disrupt Congolese unity, letting the Belgians continue to rule the country by a "divide and conquer" policy.

He shot off a telegram to Minister De Schrijver demanding that the December elections be postponed until they could be enlarged in consultation with the M.N.C. De Schrijver refused. Lumumba angrily called an M.N.C. Congress at the Congo's third largest city, Stanleyville (Oriental Province).

On October 27, enthusiastic native crowds roared a welcome to the white convertible that brought the return of a popular hero to the city where he had begun his political career.

Cheering his attacks on DeSchrijver, the M.N.C. Congress lined up behind his demand for a boycott of the December elections. A stir of excitement ran through the city when Lumumba urged the "oppressed people of the Congo to mobilize themselves to put an end to Belgian domination."

Racial tension was already high in Stanleyville, where 5,000 European plantation owners, merchants and government employees lived in segregated splendor. Evolués, riding bicycles and living in small brick houses, resented the beautiful homes, cars, splendid clothes and servants of the whites. The black masses, living in mud huts with not even bicycles, regarded the affluent whites with open hatred.

On the final day of the congress Lumumba, speaking in a tribal tongue, called on Africans to "drive out the Europeans" as the cause of all their troubles. Once the whites had been kicked out, he promised, life in Stanleyville would be all milk and honey. There would be little need to work, no taxes to pay, plenty of money for everybody and a division of the white man's property among the Congolese.

His demagoguery worked up a mood of near hysteria in his listeners. Surging from the meeting, they set fire to buildings in the European sector of the city. The Force Publique sealed off the sector and sent for an armored division with nine tanks. The mob attacked advancing troops and police with stones, spears and arrows. Troops hurled teargas, then opened fire. Before the riot was quelled, 26 Congolese were killed and over a hundred Africans and Europeans were wounded.

A warrant was issued for Lumumba's arrest, charging him with inciting the riot. Going into hiding, he slipped from place to place whenever "talking drums" warned him of the approach of police. But he was finally seized, tried and sentenced to six months in jail. Crowds gathered daily outside the prison for news of him. New thousands joined the M.N.C., assured that membership cards would entitle them to special privileges in Lumumba's promised paradise.

The approach of the December elections intensified tribal conflict. Struggles broke out within bush tribes as well, as a youthful new guard sought to wrest positions of leadership from old chiefs. Witch doctors, seeking to hold on to their old power, revived ancient fears of the *mundele ya mwinda*— the slave-hunter whose lantern had hypnotized victims.

The myth was modernized to create superstitious dread of the car headlights of politicians who drove around the Congo in preparation for the elections. Many cars were attacked and their occupants dragged out and beaten or killed.

Fresh fighting flared around Luluabourg as the Bena Lulua and the Baluba campaigned against each other in Kasai. The Bena Lulua insisted that ancient tribal ways be preserved. The Baluba, allied with Kalonji's M.N.C., demanded that Kasai move forward into the 20th century. Attacking undefended Baluba communes, the Bena Lulua burned huts and massacred 500 Baluba over a 40-mile area.

Without consulting the Belgian Parliament, King Baudoin left for the Congo, hoping to repeat his earlier triumphant tour and calm things down. Three days before the local elections he arrived in Stanleyville, only to be met by hostile M.N.C. mobs demanding Lumumba's release. He had to be rescued by Force Publique troops using teargas. Local Congolese leaders warned the shaken king that unless Belgium granted independence immediately, Leopoldville and Stanleyville would explode.

He prudently retreated to nearby Ruanda-Urundi, a Congo mandate, as voting began on December 20. For four days an estimated 1,870,000 Congolese went to the polls. To the surprise of everyone concerned, the elections came off without violence or bloodshed. From Stanleyville prison Lumumba had revoked an M.N.C. boycott against the election, ordering his followers to demonstrate M.N.C. strength in ballots.

The M.N.C. swept the elections in Oriental Province, taking 55 out of 73 seats on the new councils, the greatest triumph of any party in the Congo. In Kasai Province, Kalonji's M.N.C. came out ahead, but by only a small margin. In Katanga, Tshombe's CONAKAT won an easy victory. In Leopoldville, where Kasavubu's ABAKO had boycotted the elections, and in Equator and Kivu Provinces, the campaigns were won by local candidates unaffiliated with any major parties.

Hundreds of splinter parties that had surfaced hopefully in the crest of the election disappeared in its wake.

Kasavubu called a special ABAKO Congress at Kisantu in the Lower Congo, inviting Kalonji's M.N.C. and some smaller parties to enter a coalition to oppose Lumumba's drive for a strong republic. Kasavubu called for immediate independence as a loose federation of all-powerful provinces.

He asked Belgium to stop its capitalists from withdrawing their profits from the Congo, so that Congolese might have "an equitable division of the national revenue." To make this demand palatable he flattered the Belgians as a "courageous and proud people, people who have never recoiled before great sacrifices . . . people profoundly Christian and good."

But many Belgian investors saw the approach of independence as a forerunner of government confiscation, and began liquidating their property and businesses. Union Miniere officials, alarmed by Kasavubu's hints and Lumumba's anti-Europeanism, redoubled their support of Tshombe.

Great wealth was at stake in the Congo. Since World War II foreign investments had increased by 11 billion francs a year in commerce, banking, transportation, mines, manufacturers and plantations. The Congo's principal customer was Belgium, which took a fourth of the colony's products; next was the United States, which took a fifth. Union Miniere had increased its Congo profits from 600 million francs a year at war's end to 4.5 billion francs annually by the elections.

Industrialists of many countries were worried; they had a vital interest in the future of the Congo. It now supplied 90 per cent of the world's industrial diamonds, vital to all manufacturing processes. Ranking first in the supply of cobalt, it was fourth in copper and tin, sixth in zinc and palm oil and an important producer of rare metals like tantalum and manganese. Would a black Congo republic of half-educated, largely untrained administrators be able to maintain this production? Might they not, out of hostility to the white West, turn instead to the Communist East for their trade?

At stake, too, were investments in an elaborate transportation system to extract the riches of the Congo—over 8,700 miles of navigable waterways served by 1,500 boats; 3,000 miles of railroad track traveled by 8,000 freight cars; 90,000 miles of road driven by 50,000 vehicles; a 22,000-mile airline system tying together key cities.

Matadi, leading seaport of the Congo, was connected to

Leopoldville by rail. Through Matadi flowed two or three million tons of valuable cargoes a year.

Uncertainty now shrouded the fate of this vast industrial empire. There was good reason to dread a "revolution of rising expectations," as Adlai Stevenson called it. ABAKO, in boycotting the 1959 elections, had sent its party officials an ominous secret memo:

"Don't forget that as of the evening of December 31, 1959, there will no longer be any authority over us, even colonial authority. We will fall into anarchy again, but this time under the direction of . . . ABAKO!"

After the elections the Bakongo ignored Belgian officials and newly elected Africans. Most of the Lower Congo slipped under the de facto control of Kasavubu.

In Stanleyville the victory of Lumumba's M.N.C. was followed by new acts of hostility toward the European population. Roads were blocked by logs, tires punctured, white drivers stoned. White homes were burglarized, purses snatched. African servants were frightened out of white employ by rumors that they would be killed after independence.

Stanleyville seethed with whispers of the terrible fate in store for Europeans when the Government became black.

Whenever whites ventured from their beautiful homes, women as well as men took to carrying revolvers.

# 7
# An Astonishing Surrender

DESPITE LUMUMBA'S TRIUMPH at the polls, he was sentenced to six months in prison, his second jail term, for having incited the Stanleyville riots. Fearful of an attempt by his followers to free him, Belgian authorities cautiously transferred him to Jadotville prison in Katanga, where the Lunda had little love for him.

The ferment and violence in the Congo made millions of Belgians question the wisdom of trying to hang on to it forcibly. They dreaded finding themselves in the predicament of France, with another costly, bloody and unwinnable Algerian or Vietnam war on their hands. Demonstrators began picketing Parliament, warning: NOT ONE SOLDIER FOR THE CONGO!

"I asked a man who is quite possibly the single most powerful living Belgian," reported American journalist John Gunther, "how long Belgium could hold the Congo, how long the rule of the white man was going to last. He replied, 'Sooner or later we will have to have elections. After that, five years.'"

Parliament decided that the most prudent course lay in

79

conciliating Lumumba and the other Congo politicians who were demanding independence immediately, not in 1964.

On January 20, 1960, all Congolese leaders were summoned to a Round Table Conference in Brussels to discuss when and how independence should come to the Congo.

A wave of amazement swept through the Congo. For most African politicians "Independence Now!" had been purely a slogan for stirring black emotions and winning votes. None, not even Lumumba, had really believed that the Belgian Government—with a vast $4 billion investment at stake—would yield so quickly to Congolese demands for a joint conference to work out plans for speeding their freedom. Many evolués went to Brussels suspecting a trick or delaying tactic.

The M.N.C., however, notified De Schrijver that they would not attend the conference unless Lumumba was allowed to represent them. Since a meaningful conference without the M.N.C. was impossible, Lumumba was freed from jail to go to Brussels. Asked by a conference hall guard for his credentials, Lumumba ironically displayed the handcuff scars on his wrists.

The 81 Congolese delegates to the Round Table Conference, representing 62 political parties and 19 tribal associations or chiefs, commuted daily between their hotels and the conference hall in chartered streetcars. Most, seeing a white European city for the first time, were fascinated by such impressive sights as the Palais de la Nation and the Grand Palace.

De Schrijver urged the delegates to agree to some kind of Belgo-Congolese union, with strong autonomy for the provinces. His tactic, designed to protect Belgian investments, was swept aside at the outset by a unanimous conference demand for a date to be set for total and swift independence.

Even the most conservative of the delegates did not dare dissent, for fear of being branded Uncle Toms by political rivals. The Belgian Cabinet, which had called the conference, had no alternative but to yield to the ultimatum.

Parliament knew that the Belgian people would never tolerate a colonial war to block independence for the Congo. Leading Belgian intellectuals reminded their countrymen of the international denunciation and loss of prestige Belgium had suffered upon exposure of the Congo atrocities under Leopold's private rule. Could Belgium afford to alienate world opinion again by massacring Africans demanding freedom?

There was, besides, powerful pressure behind the scenes from the United States. Mindful of the rapidly growing number of new African nations in the U.N., Washington was hopeful that by using its influence to help end colonialism in the Congo, it would win African votes on key U.N. issues.

The Belgian Cabinet was nevertheless uneasy about granting independence like a Christmas package. The delegates demanding the reins of government in the Congo were something less than inspiring in their qualifications. Only a dozen of the 81 had had a college education; most had less than a high school education, often only in theological studies.

There was among them not one engineer, lawyer, architect, doctor, social scientist or economist. The Belgian policy of keeping key posts in the Congo in white hands had left the evolués deplorably untrained for self-government. But it was too late to buy time. Belgium's stubborn policy of paternalism would have to be paid for in chaos.

Lumumba's was the commanding voice at the conference. The historic occasion seemed to bring out an unexpected statesmanlike quality in him that had not been apparent in

Stanleyville, where he had played the role of political firebrand.

"The fact that Belgium has liberated the Congo from the
colonial regime we were no longer prepared to accept has
won her the friendship and esteem of the Congolese people,"
he assured his hosts cordially. "We desire this friendship to
be enduring and free of all forms of hypocrisy."

He had soothing words for all Europeans living in the
Congo: "We would ask them to stay and help the young
Congolese state. We need their help. It is with their collabo-
ration that we wish to create the Congolese nation, in which
all will find their share of happiness and satisfaction."

This new, strangely reasonable and mild Lumumba, heading the strongest political party in the Congo, appealed to
the Brussels Cabinet as perhaps the best chance to establish
a stable republic as well as protect Belgian interests.

The Belgians knew Kasavubu to be a separatist seeking to
establish a Bakongo empire, with Communist aid if necessary.
Kalonji was distrusted as a fomenter of tribal war in the
Kasai. Tshombe, considered a safe tool of Union Miniere,
had no support outside the Province of Katanga, and even
there was fiercely opposed by Jason Sendwe's Baluba.

The Belgian Cabinet was well aware of a telegram sent to
Tshombe at the conference from 32 influential whites of
Katanga: "IF THERE IS A STALEMATE AT THE ROUND
TABLE, WE STAND BEHIND YOU FOR A FUTURE
INDEPENDENT KATANGA." De Schrijver listened thought-
fully to Lumumba's argument that only a strong united Congo
republic, which had the power to pool the wealth of all the
provinces, could possibly survive.

Would such a republic, Lumumba was asked, be willing to

grant Belgium three military bases to protect Belgian lives and property? It would, he replied promptly, in exchange for absolute independence with Belgian technical and economic assistance under African direction.

Kasavubu, angered by his failure to win support for a loosely federated republic that would assure Bakongo autonomy, withdrew from the conference in a huff. When he returned he found to his dismay that the Belgian Cabinet, despite anguished outcries from wealthy Belgian investors and Tshombe, was ready to sign a treaty based on the understanding reached with Lumumba. On June 30, 1960, the Congo would become an independent nation under its own flag.

Even Kasavubu's own lieutenant, Daniel Kanza, had led a revolt of ABAKO Bakongo against his walkout, voting for provincial elections in May to pave the way for the creation of a new centralized Democratic Republic of the Congo.

The Belgian press praised the Cabinet's repudiation of colonialism, based on the tardy realization that paternalism had never been good enough; that no people would consent to be treated as children forever, however well they were looked after; that sooner or later they would rebel and demand the right to run their own lives.

The Belgian Cabinet was counting hopefully on Lumumba's new attitude of sweet reasonableness, his apparent willingness to accept political advice, the treaty concessions he had made, his ability to inspire a nationalistic spirit that could override tribal rivalries and his power through popular support to preserve law and order.

"We were criticized for letting the Congolese go when they were tragically unprepared to become a nation," one Belgian official later explained. "It was true that we were shortsighted in not having prepared them for the day. But when the agitation arose for independence, we knew that we had to bend with the new winds blowing in Africa."

The Belgians, he pointed out, had tried to buy time to prepare the Congolese for independence—four years of time. "But their cry was 'Independence Now!' If we had insisted upon our plan of preparation first, we would have had a colonial war on our hands. And the whole world would have accused us of using stalling tactics to hold on to the Congo. We really had no choice but to let them go as they demanded."

The reaction in the Congo was largely one of astonishment and disbelief. "We feel like one who has been given a present that he has wanted for a long time," admitted the *Courrier d'Afrique*, "but did not dare to believe that he would get." After the first shock, joyful African celebrations broke out all over the Congo. Whites were stunned.

Wild rumors flew around Stanleyville. Any African who dared vote against M.N.C. would be known and assassinated. Europeans in the Congo were planning to wipe out the blacks by poisoning the supply of African beer. Racial tension soared, making whites afraid to be away from home after dark. Many started shipping money and valuables back home. Belgian businesses began to shut down, throwing Congolese out of work and adding to growing unrest.

The European exodus accelerated when African racketeers began "selling" white homes to gullible natives for $40 each, for occupancy after independence. There were even "sales" of colonists' wives for $20 apiece as part of the deal. Naïve Congolese began knocking on European doors asking to see the white property, real and personal, they had just bought.

One spokesman for the white colonists, R. E. Lenain, denounced the De Schrijver Cabinet for "criminal behavior." He accused Brussels of washing its hands of responsibility for the Congo, telling the colonists in effect: "We have done our duty in turning over to the Africans that which is theirs. There is nothing more for us in this affair. If you are slaughtered or pillaged, if the Congo returns to barbarism, don't complain to us. Address yourselves to your own Democratic Republic of the Congo."

The plan, Lenain charged bitterly, was "far too cowardly to succeed." The Belgian Government itself was apprehensive about the conference decision, but felt helpless to change the dynamic thrust of events.

"The only mistake the Belgians may be making," admitted *Inforcongo*, the government's mouthpiece, "is to expect . . . moderation and common sense from the self-appointed leaders. . . . Recent outbursts in the Congo . . . have demonstrated that political consciousness in the modern sense is not yet strong enough to override tribalism and feuds between races."

It also conceded, "Extreme forms of tribalism . . . are also inspiring some wholly unrealistic plans for cutting the Congo into pieces without calculating economic consequences."

The persistence of Congo tribalism on the eve of independence was no surprise to African experts in Brussels universities, who had not been consulted.

For centuries the natives had been loyal to such great tribal kingdoms as the Bakongo, the Baluba, the Lunda and the Bayeke. Tribal ties had historic meaning for most Africans, who felt nothing for the political government of the whites, from which they had been rigidly excluded. The fact that the white structure was about to turn black did not alter their tribal allegiances.

The tribal clan alone represented security for the average Congolese. If natural disaster struck a family, clansmen would feed and shelter its members, helping them build a new home. Tribesmen looked after the crippled and the aged. Those who left the clan for city jobs often felt homesick and insecure. It was this anxiety that led even evolués to join in urban tribal associations, perpetuating and strengthening their ancient tribal ties.

No Lunda rejoiced at the possibility of falling under the domination of rival Bakongo or Baluba. As the May elections drew near, tribal rivalry intensified. The major protagonists in the struggle for power were Lumumba, heading a tribal coalition in M.N.C.; Tshombe, heading CONAKAT for the Lunda; Kasavubu, heading ABAKO for the Bakongo; Kalonji, heading M.N.C.-Kalonji for the Kasai Baluba; and Sendwe, heading BALUBAKAT for the Katanga Baluba.

The country was fractured far beyond only those divisions, however. The new government would have to represent almost 200 tribes speaking over 400 different languages and dialects. French was the official language of the Congo, but less than 10 per cent of Congolese were educated enough to speak it.

Candidates for public office began barnstorming around the country in February, 1960. New to the art of politics, many solicited votes by threatening personal harm to any who opposed them. In Oriental and parts of Kasai, natives who couldn't display M.N.C. party cards were assaulted. Murders of one tribe's candidates by another's were not uncommon.

With the Belgian restraints removed, ancient tribal hatreds

surfaced explosively. Increasingly numbers of Europeans fled the country in alarm.

In Katanga, Tshombe, a splendid figure in button-down white shirt, red tie, blue tweed suit and homburg, campaigned in a black Cadillac, accompanied by a Pretorian guard of shirtsleeved toughs with *"Votez* CONAKAT" inscribed on red and white caps. He proposed a Congo republic on the order of the United States, with regionalized power.

"We are willing to share our mining revenues with the rest of the Congo," he announced, "but we want at least 50 per cent of the wealth . . . kept in Katanga."

Many black politicians wooed voters with reckless and irresponsible promises. All the white man's property—homes, cars, wives—would be turned over to Africans. Every worker would get huge pay raises and free benefits of every kind. There would be plenty of money for everybody; every African would be able to enjoy all European luxuries.

The Force Publique was kept on continuous duty during the volatile political campaigns to quell rioters, break up tribal clashes and enforce curfews. But the 23,000 Congolese enlisted men and noncoms (the force still had not a single black officer) grew increasingly restive themselves. What about *their* rights? Belgian officers told them curtly that independence affected Congolese civilians only; but a small political party gave space to their complaints in its paper, *Emancipation*: "There is no human contact between us and our officers. We are veritable slaves. We are thought of as belonging to an inferior race. The unanimous desire of all Congolese soldiers is to occupy posts of command, to earn a decent salary, to put an end to all traces of discrimination in the Force Publique." If these demands were not met, the soldiers hinted darkly, "We assure you that the independence of June 30 will be unsteady!"

But the Commander of the Force Publique, General Emile Janssens, took a dim view not only of the idea of black officers but of the whole transfer of power to "a pack of black politicians."

No African was promoted to the rank of officer.

Janssens' obstinacy received unexpected support from none other than Patrice Lumumba, who scornfully told blacks in the force, "We are not, just because the Congo will be independent, going to turn a second-class soldier into a general!"

Lumumba did not trust the ambitions of those Congolese noncoms who were reaching out for military power. Their angry reply appeared in *Emancipation* on March 19, 1960: "How shameful to say such things publicly! M. Lumumba was never in the Force Publique and will never be in it, so how can he judge that there is no one in it capable of replacing the officers? Dear Lumumba, beloved brother of the whites, . . . the hour of pushing us around like lambs is passed. We guarantee you the ruination of your powers and of your Congo so long as you insult us as ignorant people who are incapable of taking the places of your white brothers."

There was high irony in this pinning of an Uncle Tom label on the African leader who had gone to jail for inciting a race riot against the whites in Stanleyville. But Lumumba's disdain for the grievances of the rank and file in the Force Publique was to have explosive consequences.

All through March, 1960, he campaigned confidently for M.N.C. in his white convertible. Western reporters who sought to interview him found a tall, thin African with goatee and thick-lensed glasses, dressed in bow tie and tweeds, with a charismatic smile and silver tongue. One newsman observed that he moved swiftly, made snap judgments and sought quick solutions.

"His outlook," reported another, "is firmly Western."

The Belgians, tacitly grooming Lumumba for the post of prime minister of the new republic, suddenly made an unpleasant discovery in mid-April. Despite generous campaign funds made available to him by Belgian industrialists, he had been accepting money not only from Ghana, Guinea and the United Arab Republic but also from Communist East Europe.

De Schrijver reprimanded him angrily. Stung, Lumumba lashed back by accusing the Belgians of trying to control him through paternalism. What kind of independence was *that* supposed to be? The Belgians began to feel that they had made a serious misjudgment in supporting Lumumba. At the last moment they began to show interest in Kasavubu instead.

But the Belgian Communist Party, working through the Soviet Embassy in Brussels, had already arranged more than just financial aid for Lumumba. Communist advisers were arriving in Stanleyville from East Germany and Czechoslovakia, where already 125 M.N.C. leaders, including Lumumba's chief aide, Antoine Gizenga, were being given leadership training.

Communist supplies of small arms were being smuggled into M.N.C. across the northeast borders of Oriental Province.

Exposure of Lumumba's acceptance of aid from East Europe caused a new split in M.N.C. ranks. Violent clashes broke out between Lumumba's followers and an anti-Communist faction, who were led out of M.N.C. by Victor Nendaka.

Lumumba and Kasavubu both wired the new resident minister of the Congo, Ganshof van der Meersch, demanding immediate formation of a provisional government to keep order until Independence Day. Flatly refusing, Van der Meersch reinforced Belgium's military bases instead.

In angry campaign speeches Lumumba accused Brussels of secret plans to set up a puppet Congo government backed by Belgian bayonets.

Fresh violence broke out on Election Day. M.N.C. party workers in Oriental Province seized voting tickets from African hands and jammed them into boxes marked for M.N.C. ballots. Polling booths were wrecked, election officials intimidated and beaten. In Kasai, spear-carrying Baluba attacked and stabbed Bena Lulua in the streets. In Katanga, Jason Sendwe's BALUBAKAT fought fiercely with Tshombe's CONAKAT.

When the polls were finally closed, five weeks of electioneering had left about 60 dead and hundreds wounded.

Even before it had been raised, the new blue-and-gold banner of the emerging republic had been stained blood-red.

# 8
# Mutiny

THE GENERAL ELECTIONS OF MAY set up not only provincial governments but also a national Chamber of Representatives, whose 137 members reflected the various strengths of rival parties and tribes. Lumumba's M.N.C. emerged as the strongest party in the Chamber, winning 33 seats out of 137 and controlling another 31 held by smaller parties in his coalition.

His victory left Lumumba in strong control of the new Oriental Assembly as well, winning twice as many votes as his nearest rival. In the Leopoldville Assembly, Kasavubu's ABAKO held a slim majority over the P.S.A., led by Gizenga, an ally of Lumumba. The Katanga Assembly was almost equally divided between Tshombe's CONAKAT and Sendwe's BALUBAKAT, with Tshombe controlling 32 seats out of 60. In Kivu, Equator and Kasai no single parties dominated the new assemblies.

Lumumba emerged as the only leader with both national support and an overwhelming majority in his own province. He also enjoyed great personal prestige as an African patriot who had been imprisoned by the Belgians for "subversive activities." Identified with no one powerful tribe and dedicated to a "Congo United," he was an ideal compromise as national leader for many small tribes and for tribesmen who

91

feared domination of the new republic by one powerful tribe. He now had supporters in five of the six new assemblies. In the sixth—Katanga—Jason Sendwe grew convinced that Tshombe was plotting secession from the new republic. He refused to allow his BALUBAKAT deputies to take seats in the new Katanga Assembly. Sitting without them, the Lunda of CONAKAT, to no one's great surprise, named Tshombe as premier of the province. Union Miniere promptly began paying taxes, royalties and dividends into CONAKAT's coffers. Herman Robiliart, president of the company, later indignantly denied charges he had subsidized Tshombe's secession.

"Like any private enterprise anywhere, we need peace and order, not war and strife, to conduct our operations smoothly," he told American newsmen. "Those who accuse us of military adventuring assume that we are ignorant of our own self-interest. It is preposterous to suppose that a private company would engage in activities that would invite harm to its personnel or its properties."

Through Tshombe, Union Miniere persistently accused Lumumba of plotting to seize the Congo for Communism. The Soviet Union, Tshombe charged, was hungry for Katanga, which produced six tons of copper for every 11 tons mined by the whole Communist bloc. Such attacks did not go unheard in Washington.

Bachir Ben Yachmid, editor of the popular African magazine *Jeune Afrique*, later reported that the United States had decided to intervene in the Congo on the theory that Lumumba's repudiation of Belgian hegemony had created a "power vacuum eyed enviously by the Soviet Union."

Tshombe did not have much difficulty in getting his Lunda

tribesmen to support his policy of cooperating with the white industrialists who ran Union Miniere. The company's paternalism had many black champions in Katanga.

Unlike South Africa's diamond mines, where natives were forced to work away from their wives and children, Union Miniere provided good housing at the mines, without cost, for workers' families. Over 22,000 Congolese children attended schools managed or financed by Union Miniere, and taught by 700 company-trained African teachers. School lunches for children included milk, hot meals and cod liver oil.

Adult education classes were held for 3,300 black workers, of whom 390 were at last being trained for junior executive or supervisor posts. The company also provided free medical facilities for everyone in Katanga, black and white alike, at excellent hospitals and dispensaries. Union Miniere's workers also enjoyed family allowances, paid vacations, old-age pensions and the highest wages in Africa.

But if the whites in Katanga counted on Tshombe to protect their interests when the Congo became a republic, Europeans in other provinces were less optimistic. All through May and June of 1960, Belgium's Sabena Airlines was booked solidly with flights of departing whites. Sabena had to borrow planes to meet a huge new wave of demands for plane tickets when the colonial government, fearing financial collapse, forbade residents to send more than $200 a month out of the country. The exodus from the Congo swelled steadily.

Belgian civil servants and businessmen who headed home left severe gaps in an economy that had no trained replacements for them. Would a self-governing Congo be able to survive without them? "Whether independence works or not," Kasavubu insisted, "there is no question of delaying it."

As Independence Day, June 30, drew closer, Lumumba jockeyed furiously for power, seeking new coalitions which would guarantee his control of the new Congo republic. His pre-eminence in the May elections forced Minister Van der Meersch to authorize him to be the first to try to form a cabinet that could command majority support.

To Lumumba's despair, Kasavubu would not agree on how the portfolios of the new cabinet should be shared. After only four days of negotiations, Lumumba was abruptly dismissed by Van der Meersch, who turned the task over to Kasavubu.

Bitterly accusing Van der Meersch and Brussels of conspiracy against him, Lumumba threatened to boycott all participation in the new government. But Kasavubu was even less successful in forming a ministry, so Van der Meersch had no choice but to offer Lumumba another opportunity. With only nine days to go before Independence Day, the embarrassed Belgians still had no native government to whom it could transfer its colony as a republic, as it was sworn to do.

Lumumba engaged in some whirlwind wheeling and dealing to win enough support from splinter parties to form a majority coalition. Small tribes bargained their votes for promises of cabinet or government posts. Lumumba played off one against the other, inadvertently intensifying tribal rivalries. Finally he compromised his differences with Kasavubu by offering him the presidency of the new republic, and on June 23 he had enough votes to form a government.

Although Kasavubu would be President, the lion's share of power would rest with Lumumba as Prime Minister. On June 29, Lumumba signed a treaty with Belgium spelling out the terms agreed upon at the Round Table Conference in Brussels. Jubilant at his victory, he still chafed at what he considered a last-minute attempt by the Belgians to dump him.

Tshombe, who had been derided by Lumumba for showing up at Leopoldville with white advisers, was chagrined by his rival's success in putting together an M.N.C.-ABAKO coalition. He agreed to participate in the new government, however, if CONAKAT were offered the ministries of economic affairs, defense and state. His party, he argued, deserved a share of power commensurate with Katanga's major importance in the Congo's economy.

It was obvious to Lumumba and Kasavubu that Tshombe hoped to use those portfolios to protect Union Miniere from encroachment of its wealth by the new republic. They joined together to outwit him. The Defense Ministry, Tshombe was informed, had already been given to Colonel Joseph Mobutu, a Kasavubu supporter. However, he could become Minister of Economic Affairs. Tshombe accepted grudgingly.

After his participation in Lumumba's Cabinet had been announced, he was shocked to discover that he had been shrewdly outwitted. Lumumba and Kasavubu had watered down his powers by appointing two M.N.C. officials as Ministers of "Economic Coordination and Planning" and "External Commerce." Both portfolios could be used to thwart his regionalism.

Tshombe returned home to Elizabethville frustrated and embittered. He was also furious at fellow Katangan Jason Sendwe for having allied BALUBAKAT with M.N.C.-ABAKO.

Lumumba now found himself with an unwieldy cabinet of 37 members, 16 of whom represented different parties. He also knew that he would not have an easy time carrying out his program for a united Congo republic with a President whose goal had always been a separate Bakongo kingdom.

It was hardly the most auspicious beginning for a fragile new republic bewildered by complex problems and responsibilities. To make the situation worse, Independence Day had brought in its wake a week of riots and mutiny by the Force Publique. Then Tshombe and the Province of Katanga had seceded, pulling out the republic's financial props.

The stormy events of the first 11 days of the new Democratic Republic of the Congo, described in the first chapter, made it seem extremely unlikely that the star-crossed new African nation could survive. With government operations collapsing all around him, Lumumba knew it was imperative to find a way to stop the flight of the remaining Europeans. Without them the new republic would be like an airliner flying into a violent storm with no one in the cockpit.

But white officials in the Congo lived in a climate of terror. Force Publique mutineers were unleashing their long-festering hatred of white officers on all Europeans, women as well as men. The number of attacks, rapes and murders, however, was vastly exaggerated by hysterical rumors. At first, whites were more often humiliated than hurt by hostile Congolese. At Matadi, for example, a group of white women were dragged out to a savannah and forced at gunpoint to cut grass barefoot like native women, then were let go.

The native mood turned uglier when the Belgian Government flew in paratroops to rescue beseiged whites, and in the process indiscriminately opened fire on Africans.

The "paras," patrolling Matadi and Leopoldville at night, shot at anything that moved. Mutinous troops in the Matadi garrison were pounded by grenades, mortars and machine guns.

Inflamed, Force Publique units in other parts of the country sought revenge by seizing and mistreating whites of both sexes. A subsequent Belgian Commission of Inquiry established a total of 52 cases of rape during this period of anarchy. The Western press dramatized them in huge black headlines, but almost completely ignored the much larger number of atrocities committed by paratroops against Congolese. Some reporters felt that the Belgian intervention had actually cost many more lives, white and black, than it had saved.

In Lumumba's suspicious eyes, the true mission of the paratroops had not been to rescue whites, but to serve as an advance guard of reinforcements for Belgium's military bases in the Congo. Belgian troops, he was convinced, would be used to protect Union Miniere and defend the secession of Katanga, possibly to the point of mounting a civil war under Tshombe to topple the Lumumba-Kasavubu regime.

Tshombe publicly called upon Belgium to send him more troops to protect his province from the disorders breaking out in the rest of the country. Declaring Katanga an independent nation, he branded Lumumba a Communist and appealed for the recognition and help of all Western anti-Communist powers.

He had both legal and moral justification for withdrawing Katanga from the Congo Union, Tshombe insisted. The Lunda had always been a tribe apart, with separate traditions of language, history, communications and development. The Belgian Congo had been created by cutting across tribal lines, creating an artificial country united only by colonial rule.

Tshombe challenged the right of other tribes, coalesced under Lumumba and Kasavubu, to dictate to the Lunda that they must submit to a strong central government that perpetu-

97

ated "this fictitious nation." He had been willing to accept a loose federation of provinces, he pointed out, but not the yoking of Katanga to a "Communist-dominated Leopoldville."

Raising the green, white and red flag of an independent Katanga, Tshombe began printing his own money and stamps. He won quick agreement from Union Miniere to reopen its mines. Elizabethville was flooded with posters: KATANGA DEFENDS AFRICA AGAINST COMMUNISM! The Force Publique was purged of all non-Katangais and anti-Tshombe elements, even though this left his 200 white Belgian officers with only 200 native troops. Replacements quickly came from Lunda tribesmen.

Faced with Tshombe's secession, Lumumba knew that he had no choice but to persuade or compel the rebel leader to return to the fold, or to overthrow him. Without revenues from Union Miniere, the Government's budget would be slashed in half. Even more dangerous, other tribal leaders in the Cabinet might be encouraged to follow Tshombe's example. One of the first abdicators, in fact, might be President Kasavubu.

At Lumumba's insistence, Kasavubu agreed to fly with him to Elizabethville to reason with Tshombe. But their plane was refused landing clearance, and they were forced to return to Leopoldville. They were a little stunned to find that in their brief absence the Cabinet had decided to appeal to Washington for aid in restoring order to the still out-of-control Force Publique, now the National Congolese Army (A.N.C.).

President Dwight D. Eisenhower cautiously advised the Congolese to apply for help instead to the U.N. Lumumba decided to take his advice. With the A.N.C. a shambles of disunity, he was completely at the mercy of any military thrust from Katanga by Belgian troops intent upon unseating him.

If the U.N. failed to act to support the integrity of a member nation, Lumumba warned the Security Council, then what other small nation in the U.N. could count upon its protection? He turned a scornfully deaf ear to hints by Western nations that their U.N. support for his republic might depend on his willingness to shut the door on any Communist help.

As an African whose country had long been exploited by Western colonialism but not by any Communist power, Lumumba considered that the demands of the West came with poor grace and worse tact. His frame of mind was that of other African leaders whose countries were emerging from colonialism.

"If they hated their colonial rulers," explained Professor Lucian W. Pye, American social psychologist, "then they cannot expect to find their identities by following the same path." A Congo nationalist to his bones, Lumumba was determined to follow his own path in creating a strong African nation. Western support alone had never brought independence to the Congo. Why should it alone be entrusted with sustaining independence now?

Thus, while demanding aid from the Western-dominated U.N., he also sought aid from the Communist bloc. He fully trusted no white men, whether from East or West. His erratic moods, often triggered by suspicion because he was never sure whom to believe, made him unpredictable. His political compass gyrated wildly depending on whether East or West seemed to be offering the most useful aid in preserving the republic.

Much of the Western press was hostile toward him.

"Leaving the country civil-war torn," wrote Smith Hempstone, African correspondent of the Chicago *Daily News*, "he embarked on a junket to Britain, North Africa, the United States and Canada. While Congolese died, he inspected Cadillacs in Washington and associated with a red-haired Belgian girl." Hempstone also accused him of black racism: "When Lumumba's hard won but thin veneer of culture failed to open the gate to success, power and acclaim, he found the cause of failure not in himself but in the white man's duplicity."

The highly volatile situation in the Congo was not helped by Lumumba's unstable personality and his hunger for the trappings of power. But it was understandable that a poor, self-educated tribal boy who had twice been jailed in a stormy struggle to the black heights of a white-controlled society should find his political success intoxicating.

There were renewed rumors that he had made a secret deal with Moscow to give the Soviet Union hegemony in the Congo. *Time* magazine branded three M.N.C. officials as having "obvious Red leanings." The Belgian Government called the mutiny of the A.N.C. a Communist plot to wreck the Congo, with Lumumba's connivance. Tshombe accused Lumumba of seeking to establish "a ruinous and Communist state."

"We are not Communists, Catholics or Socialists," Lumumba replied scornfully. "We are African nationalists." The Congo Republic, he vowed, would choose its friends "according to the principle of positive neutrality." He waited for word from U.N. General Secretary Dag Hammarskjöld as to that world organization's willingness to come to his rescue. Meanwhile, he also consulted the Soviet Ambassador to Leopoldville about the U.S.S.R.'s offers of support for the new republic.

Hammarskjöld found himself on the horns of a dilemma. A

quick agreement to back Lumumba would antagonize many West European powers with holdings in Katanga. But if Lumumba's request for help were to be stalled in routine U.N. diplomatic channels, the Democratic Republic of the Congo might collapse in chaos. Tshombe was hiring white mercenaries for his army and seeking Western support for an independent Katanga.

If he succeeded in getting away with it, the Congo Republic would be likely to fly apart into six separate nations, with tribal wars raging in each one for supremacy.

Hammarskjöld determined to press for a U.N. military force that could replace Belgian troops in the Congo and assist in the maintenance of order. This special force would include only troops from African countries and other smaller nations, not from any of the great powers.

Washington considered its position. Sending American troops to the Congo was out of the question, since this would open the way for the Soviet Union to do the same. Lumumba had made it clear that he would accept military aid from all countries willing to help him. If he were allowed to fall and the whole Congo splintered into tribal pieces, the U.S.S.R. could be expected to pick up some of those pieces.

So the Eisenhower Administration prudently decided that the safest course was to support Hammarskjöld's call for a neutral U.N. force to keep peace in a unified Congo.

Meanwhile, Belgian paratroops continued to attack A.N.C. forces in Leopoldville and Matadi. On July 12, 1960, Lumumba and Kasavubu, exasperated by the U.N.'s failure to respond swiftly to their call for help, wired Khrushchev for a promise of Soviet aid if the Belgian "aggression" did not stop.

Khrushchev promptly called a press conference and accused the Western powers in NATO of plotting to reduce the Congo to a colony again through the intervention of Belgian troops. He promised full Soviet "sympathies and assistance" for Lumumba, castigating Tshombe as a colonial stooge. The attempt to overthrow the Congo Republic, Khrushchev charged, was part of an imperialistic attempt to preserve Africa for colonialism.

The following day Lumumba demanded that all Belgian troops be confined to their bases, in accordance with the Congo-Belgian treaty. The Belgians ignored his demand. He and Kasavubu broke off relations and sped an urgent cable to Hammarskjöld warning that unless the U.N. sent immediate military assistance, they would get the help they needed "elsewhere."

Hammarskjöld knew that he had to act at once when Moscow growled, "The Soviet Government warns of the grave responsibilities borne by the leading circles of the Western powers for unleashing armed aggression in the Congo, and demands that it should be stopped immediately."

If the Belgians were not forced to withdraw, the Soviet Union would have a valid excuse to send troops to the new republic's aid. That in turn could lead to U.S. and British forces being sent to the Congo as a countermove. Africa might then become a new battleground of the Cold War—a confrontation that could quickly become a hot world war.

Under the authority of a U.N. Charter proviso requiring him to take action when international peace and security were endangered, Hammerskjöld called an emergency meeting of the U.N. Security Council.

# 9
# Chaos in the Congo

A BITTER DEBATE ENSUED BETWEEN the U.S. and U.S.S.R. delegates, who attacked each other acridly until 3:00 in the morning. Hammerskjöld finally coaxed them to agree on a resolution calling upon Belgium to withdraw her troops, and authorizing military assistance to the Congo Republic. The Belgian Ambassador to the U.N. promised that his country's troops would leave the Congo as quickly as a U.N. force could take over and establish order.

Working all night, Hammarskjöld raised a polyglot U.N. army of 3,500 men. Promises of troops within three days came from small neutral nations like Ghana, Tunisia, Morocco, Guinea, Mali and Ethiopia. The first contingents, arriving in Leopoldville on July 15, were organized into a U.N. command under Major General Carl Carlsson von Horn of Sweden.

Meanwhile, Lumumba, uncertain how much he could depend upon Hammarskjöld and the U.N. to save his government, asked both Peking and Moscow to follow developments closely and be prepared to come to his aid if necessary. Chou En-lai quickly agreed. Khrushchev publicly vowed that the Soviet Union would act if "aggression against the Congo" did not stop.

Washington accused Khrushchev of "intemperate, misleading and irresponsible" remarks. Brussels charged that Lumumba's appeal to Red China and the U.S.S.R. proved that he was a Communist. Lumumba denied it hotly, denouncing the Belgians for plotting to kill both him and Kasavubu.

Tshombe warned that he did not need or want U.N. troops in Katanga, and had no intention of allowing them in.

With the tensions in the Congo growing more explosive, Hammarskjöld ordered General Von Horn to use U.N. troops with absolute neutrality. They would not intervene in the Congo's internal affairs, he announced; nor would they be used to end Katanga's secession. Lumumba grew freshly suspicious.

Didn't the U.N. have a moral obligation to uphold his government as the only legal authority in the Congo? It did not escape his notice that most U.N. troops and supplies airlifted to the Congo were flown in by U.S. Army planes. Was the U.N. intervention, he wondered skeptically, really a disguised American scheme to keep Katanga and its riches safe for the West through Tshombe, while denying the U.S.S.R. access to them through Lumumba?

Most of Katanga's 8,000 whites who had fled to Rhodesia had returned, Lumumba also noted. The mines were working, the shops were open and Union Miniere was conducting business as usual, while the rest of the Congo was still in turmoil. How could they be so confident unless they had secret assurances from Hammarskjöld that Katanga would be kept independent?

But Tshombe took a vastly different view of the U.N. army. Despite Hammarskjöld's assurances of neutrality, he saw it as a threat to his secession. There was no disorder in Katanga.

Why, then, should U.N. troops seek to cross its borders unless they intended to seize the province for Lumumba?

Because Belgium had been forced to let U.N. troops supplant its own forces, Tshombe knew that he would have to rely on his own army for protection. So he began spending heavily from Katanga's treasury, fat with receipts from Union Miniere, to hire thousands of white mercenaries.

Everywhere but in Katanga the economy of the Congo was threatened with collapse. General Von Horn's forces found themselves struggling in a morass of administrative breakdowns, cobwebbed machinery, disrupted communications, stalled trains, strikes, food shortages and epidemics. Hammarskjöld rushed a U.N. civilian staff of technicians to the Congo. Scraped together from the U.N.'s specialist organizations and speaking 40 different languages, they mounted a superhuman effort to keep the new republic operative as a nation.

To add to the confusion, Von Horn clashed with Ralph Bunche, who represented Hammarskjöld in Leopoldville, over the proper way to restore order to the Congo. Von Horn favored a strictly military solution. But Bunche insisted that a political solution would automatically solve the military question. He prepared a three-page document of guidelines for the conduct of U.N. troops toward Congolese civilians.

"Some of these soldiers, I told him, came from remote villages in the Moroccan hills," the exasperated Von Horn later related, "or from the bush districts of African states where the schoolhouse had as yet made little impact. Faced with a hostile crowd, it was hardly likely they would remember Ralph's document—let alone thumb their way through pages of legalistic documents. What was vital were clear, concise orders, which could be issued by word of mouth and memorized."

The problem was crucial. Many overwrought Congolese confused the U.N. troops with the Belgian forces, and mobs often attacked a U.N. unit before they could be made to understand. But U.N. forces were under strict orders not to open fire first, except in absolute self-defense.

At Thysville one U.N. squad led by a nervous Moroccan corporal was surrounded by a threatening mob. After warning them back, he ordered his squad to open fire. A Congolese was killed and the mob scattered. Lumumba, outraged, demanded that the corporal be court-martialed. When King Mohammed of Morocco learned that the court-martial had imposed a death sentence, he instantly granted the doomed corporal a full pardon, sergeant's stripes and a medal.

Most bloody clashes in the Congo, despite lurid reports in the American press, did not involve white or black civilians but military forces. Much of the fighting took place between U.N. units and mutinous A.N.C. troops. The whites attacked were largely Belgian troops and officials.

Missionaries interviewed by *New York Times* correspondent Henry Tanner on July 14 assured him that they had not been molested. Tanner reported that he and two other newspapermen had been threatened as presumed Belgians until they proved they were Americans. That, he wrote, "unbelievably turned a mob into a laughing, cheering crowd that pressed forward to hug the Americans and shake their hands."

Lumumba, meanwhile, grew increasingly skeptical of Hammarskjöld's intentions. On July 17 he fired an angry ultimatum at the Secretary General. If the U.N. didn't get all Belgian troops out of the Congo within 72 hours, he would ask Soviet forces to do the job. Two days later the U.S.S.R. demanded a new Security Council meeting. Belgium warned that a ship from Communist Poland was en route to Leopoldville with 300 tons of munitions. Poland denied that the cargo was military.

Feeling time running out on him, Tshombe desperately appealed to Kivu and Kasai to join with Katanga in an anti-Communist alliance. The ploy failed. Then a vanguard of A.N.C. forces under General Lundula speared south into Katanga as far as Jadotville, threatening Elizabethville. Tshombe counterattacked fiercely with mercenaries. The federal troops were scattered and Lundula captured.

Tshombe feared that killing or holding Lundula might give the U.N. army an excuse for invading Katanga, so he simply expelled his prisoner from his "independent nation."

General Von Horn found his thin U.N. forces called upon to perform an almost superhuman task. They were expected to pacify an area larger than all of Western Europe, spreading across crocodile-infested rivers and tropical jungles. Their far-flung units were isolated from each other by a communications system that had collapsed with the Belgian exodus.

Faced with these problems, Ralph Bunche lost patience with Lumumba's arrogant ultimatums. He warned Lumumba not to sabotage the U.N.'s efforts by calling for Soviet troops.

Lumumba tested black sentiment. He found little enthusiasm for Russian intervention in the Congo Senate. Other African leaders warned him that a Soviet expedition would provoke an American expedition, and then Africa would be dragged into the Cold War. So Lumumba cautiously decided to ask Moscow only for an airlift of food and supplies.

But the Congo Senate endorsed his demand that Belgium get all of its troops out of the country immediately. They were being slowly pulled back to Belgian bases wherever thin U.N. units were able to fly in and establish garrisons. Belgian civilians angrily insisted that the U.N. forces were inadequate and impermanent. Brussels agreed to keep troops at Belgian bases in the Congo "as long as necessary."

Von Horn himself, despite his orders, believed that a swift evacuation of Belgian troops would only weaken chances of restoring peace to the Congo. He also deplored the refusal of the Congo Senate to ratify the treaty of friendship with Belgium. How could the new republic or his own U.N. operations succeed without Belgian technical help?

He nevertheless supported Ralph Bunche's efforts to work out a compromise. The Belgians agreed to a gradual evacuation of their troops, and Lumumba grudgingly agreed to give the U.N. a chance to get all Belgian forces out of the Congo by July 24. When Bunche also announced that troops from Canada, Italy, Burma and Ireland were arriving to strengthen the U.N. army, the threat of Soviet intervention faded.

Meanwhile, the commanders of the U.N. units that fanned out through the Congo were forced to rely more on bluff than on military strength. Battalions of 250 men sought to restore law and order to areas nearly the size of France. Most were cut off from help in case their authority was challenged. Von Horn counted on the prestige of the U.N. alone to deter tribal, political and racial troublemakers.

But crises came thick and fast. Both Belgian civilians and A.N.C. forces, caught in outbreaks of tribal fighting, appealed desperately for help. The issues were often hopelessly complicated. Commanders of U.N. rescue forces flew to trouble spots armed only with the vague instruction: "Do what seems common sense!" But what was common sense in Stanleyville, a Lumumba stronghold, was apt to prove suicidal in Albertville, a Tshombe outpost, and vice versa.

To complicate matters even more, Communist-trained guerrillas infiltrated into the Congo to provide military leadership for some of Lumumba's A.N.C. forces.

Lumumba kept insisting that Hammarskjöld was obligated to oust Tshombe and put Katanga forcibly under federal control. Hammarskjöld's refusal to take sides in the political struggle led Lumumba to accuse him wrathfully of being a "colonialist stooge." In a fit of hysteria Lumumba demanded the withdrawal of all U.N. forces except African troops, and ordered Lundula to attack them if they did not evacuate.

Declaring a national emergency, he ordered the expulsion of the Belgian Embassy and suspended free speech and assembly.

Some American newspapers suspected that the chaos in the Congo was being deliberately engineered by Brussels.

"There are many who believe," declared the Chicago *Daily News*, "that the Belgians, by their precipitate action in freeing the Congo, intended only to demonstrate its incompetence at self-government, and 'prove' the necessity for returning it to the status of a colony."

On the other hand, the Belgians had justification for suspecting the Russians of trying to replace them in the Congo.

"By September several hundred Soviet 'technicians' were in Leopoldville," reported liberal historian Arthur M. Schlesinger, former aide to President John Kennedy, "Russian military equipment was going to Lumumba's army, and communist sympathizers were moving into the central government. Lumumba obviously preferred this to assistance from the United Nations."

On July 20, Lumumba suddenly shook off all restraints and appealed openly for help from the Soviet Union, Red China or any sympathetic Afro-Asian country.

"I will make a pact with the devil himself to get the Belgians out!" he swore furiously. An uproar broke out in the Congo Senate as outraged members moved to censure him for "Communist-leaning dictatorial demands and ultimatums." He defied them, insisting that if the U.N. opposed Soviet intervention in the Congo, "it would be proof that there is a capitalist plot against the Congo!"

At the U.N. Thomas Kanza supported Lumumba's position with a passionate attack on Belgian colonialism.

"Mr. Kanza," replied Belgian Foreign Minister Pierre Wigny, "do you believe that if we had prepared any plots or any aggressions, we would have been capable of being such traitors so without honor with respect to our women, our daughters, our granddaughters, as to leave them in such a hell?"

Neither Belgians nor the Congolese people were responsible for atrocities in the Congo, Wigny declared. "The fact is that a mutinous group was not under your control, and that your government did nothing . . . to regain control over them."

"The Congolese Government," Kanza admitted, "is prepared to recognize that abuses have been committed." But he immediately added, "if I went into a recital of all the atrocities committed by the Belgians against the Congolese it would not be an edifying thing to do. . . . We are very young in international affairs, but the first example given to us by Belgium is that when you sign a treaty you . . . violate it!"

A rift between Red China and the Soviet Union over the U.N. intervention raised diplomatic eyebrows. Peking denounced it as a violation of Congo sovereignty. But Moscow suddenly softened its opposition and provided planes to assist in airlifting U.N. troops and supplies to General Von Horn.

By this time the Congolese A.N.C. army had split into four contentious groups. There were the troops under Gizenga in Stanleyville; the Tshombe forces in Elizabethville; a Kalonji contingent in Kasai; and troops loyal to Lumumba in Leopoldville and Equator Provinces.

Lumumba had found it impossible to unify the A.N.C. behind the republic because the mutiny and subsequent Africanization of the army had shifted power to the enlisted ranks. They now had the power to dismiss their officers without notice, and to elect new officers democratically. This change intensified local tribal loyalties at the expense of any vague devotion to a vague republic.

The A.N.C. had to be disarmed, Von Horn was convinced, before stability could return to the Congo. He ordered all A.N.C. units to hand over their arms to his U.N. troops. Lundula's A.N.C. forces were outraged at being stigmatized as unreliable.

Some obeyed Von Horn's edict; others bolted into the bush, especially after Lumumba furiously ordered all A.N.C. units to defy any U.N. troops who sought to disarm them. Instead of weakening the Government's forces, he raged, why wasn't the U.N. carrying out its original mission—to sweep Belgian troops out of the Congo as quickly as possible?

He was mollified on July 22, however, when the U.N. reaffirmed its intention to do just that, and a Western business

111

combine affirmed its faith in the permanence of the Congo Republic by signing an agreement with it that would provide $2 billion worth of aid, management and technical training. "There is no further need," Lumumba now purred happily, "for Soviet intervention."

Tshombe reacted with alarm. He quickly warned the U.N. that his own forces would keep out of Katanga any of their troops from countries "with Communist tendencies." The U.N., he insisted, must also not in any way interfere with Katanga's internal affairs. In a hopeful hint to Washington, he proposed that Lumumba's republic be reorganized as a "United States of the Congo," with Katanga as a sovereign state.

Lumumba was greatly pleased by evidence showing that every day more and more Belgian forces were leaving the country under pressure from the U.N. He decided to lobby personally at the U.N. for a new resolution authorizing Von Horn to use his troops to put down Tshombe's secession.

Flying to New York in a rare mood of cheerful optimism, he made a speech praising the U.N.'s efforts in the Congo. He even astonished Washington by adding, "We extend our compliments and friendship to President Eisenhower, and we also thank the American people for all they have done for the emancipation of the African people." The Congo's troubles, he admitted, were caused by unreadiness for independence. But the sin was Belgium's, for not preparing the evolués.

He met privately with the U.N.'s Soviet representatives. Afterwards the Russian delegation charged that American financiers had made a secret deal with Union Miniere to preserve the wealth of Katanga under Tshombe in return for investment privileges. Washington promptly denied it.

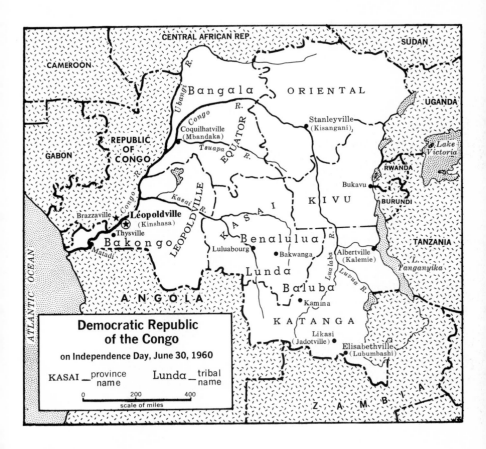

**Democratic Republic of the Congo**

on Independence Day, June 30, 1960

KASAI — province name    Lunda — tribal name

0    200    400

scale of miles

*A demonstration in Leopoldville.*

*Belgian nationals preparing to board an airline in the Congo for the flight home.*

*Moise Tschombe.*

*Premier Cyrille Adoula (center), on his way to talks with Tschombe, confers with U.N. Under-Secretary Ralph Bunche (right) and Mahmoud Khiari, Chief of U.N. Civilian Operations in the Congo.*

*Patrice Lumumba.*

*General Mobutu (second from left) inspecting U.N. troops.*

*Soldiers of the Royal Canadian 22nd Regiment training a Congolese Army officer.*

*Troops of the National Congolese Army on parade.*

*Ethiopian soldiers, who fought with the U.N. troops in the Congo, boarding a plane to return home.*

*A Canadian medical team at work in a Congolese hospital as part of the U.N. effort to maintain normal health services during the crisis.*

*Refugees who had been living in a camp under U.N. protection prepare to board trains which will take them to a new life in the traditional tribal lands of their forefathers.*

Meanwhile, in the Congo, confusion still reigned as Von Horn struggled to pacify the country with his tiny army. Belgian Ambassador M. Van den Bosch urged him to rescue 85 Belgians reported threatened by mutinous A.N.C. forces in Watsa, in Oriental Province. But Watsa was too far, and separated by impassable jungle, from the nearest U.N. forces in Stanleyville, so Von Horn cabled an appeal to Addis Ababa.

Emperor Haile Selassie promptly airlifted a company of his Ethiopian troops to the rescue. The Belgians in Watsa, however, proved to be in no danger at all, and indignantly refused to be evacuated. Outraged at having gone to all this trouble for nothing, the Ethiopian company commander forced some of them to permit him to rescue them anyhow, and compelled those who stayed behind to sign an affidavit absolving the U.N. of all responsibility for their safety.

During Lumumba's absence in New York at the U.N., Cabinet meetings in Leopoldville were presided over by his deputy, sad-faced Antoine Gizenga. To the despair of General Von Horn, who attended, the meetings were often held up by long phone calls from Gizenga's mistress, during which the other ministers would fall to squabbling among themselves. The meetings usually broke up in shouting disagreement.

"Hour after hour was wasted in this futile way," Von Horn sighed, "and I returned to the Stanley Hotel with the feeling that there was not a grain of goodwill or common sense to be found amid the politicians of Leopoldville . . . whose personal ambitions, lack of judgment, and factional and provincial rivalries were bound to have the most tragic results."

In New York the mercurial Lumumba lost his buoyant spirits as Hammarskjöld and Bunche strove patiently but

113

firmly to make him understand that he could not dictate to the U.N. how forces in the Congo were to be used. Drinking heavily and using drugs immoderately, Lumumba began flying into abusive rages against Western diplomats.

He pressed his case for overthrowing Tshombe with U.N. troops among African and Asian delegates. Encountering uneasy questions about his rumored ties to the Russians, he snapped, "I am not a Communist. I am too deeply attached to the soil of Africa!" But Hammarskjöld's decision prevailed.

On July 28 the Secretary General flew to Africa, making a futile stopover in Brussels to persuade the Belgians to withdraw all troops promptly from the Congo, including Katanga.

The Belgian Prime Minister coldly presented him with a copy of a new government report on "the brutal savagery inflicted on the white inhabitants of the Congo." The report charged that 291 Belgian women had suffered "ignoble treatment," 300 Belgian men had been "brutalized and beaten" and another 20 had been murdered.

Lumumba, frustrated by the failure of his mission in America, issued a shrill denial of these charges. But the U.S. State Department declared, "We are satisfied that the government of Belgium sent its troops to the Congo in order to protect the lives which were endangered and that it had no aggressive intent." That was enough for Lumumba.

Now bitterly convinced of a Western plot against him, he turned his back in the U.N. and determined to seek direct military aid from other African nations as well as the Communist bloc. As he had warned the West: "I will make a pact with the devil himself to get the Belgians out!"

# 10

# "The Craziest Operation in History"

HAMMARSKJÖLD ARRIVED IN LEOPOLDVILLE to find that U.N. troops in the Congo had increased to 7,500 men, still only a tiny force in a population of 14 million. In Lumumba's absence he moved swiftly to muster Congolese support for his position that U.N. forces must not intervene in the internal affairs of the country. He and General Von Horn flew to Kasavubu's home in Stanley Falls, but found the President of the Republic in agreement with Lumumba that the U.N. was obligated to enter Katanga and crush Tshombe.

When Hammarskjöld demanded that all A.N.C. units be ordered to surrender their arms to the U.N.'s peacekeeping forces, Gizenga and the Cabinet rebuked him sharply.

"The people in the Congo," Gizenga said flatly at a public reception for Hammarskjöld, "do not understand that we, against whom an aggression has been committed, we who are in our land, we who have made an appeal to international armed forces, are systematically disarmed while the Belgians, who are here in a conquered country, still have their arms and their power of death, and are simply being asked to re-

115

group in parts of our Congo some dare to call 'Belgian bases.' "

But from Katanga came warnings by Tshombe that if Hammarskjöld sent U.N. troops over the province border "it would mean war." Tshombe had sent a delegation to Brussels to negotiate recognition of Katanga's independence.

"My God!" sighed the U.N. Secretary General to Von Horn. "This is the craziest operation in history. God only knows where it is going to end!"

Meanwhile, the Congo slipped further and further into chaos. Heavy fighting between the Baluba and Bena Lulua once more erupted in Kasai. There were 400 casualties, and over 10,000 native families fled villages and towns in panic.

With only 1,646 Belgian administrators left at their posts by the end of July, government functions were in desperate shape. Most of the nation's services were at a standstill.

Under heavy U.N. pressure, Belgium began pulling troops out of all provinces except Katanga, where it refused to weaken its defenses. Hammarskjöld, who had been reluctant to seek a military solution to the problem posed by Tshombe's secession, now felt that he had no choice. He announced that U.N. forces would enter Katanga on August 6 "in accordance with the U.N. Security Council resolution calling for withdrawal of Belgian forces throughout the Congo."

"They will have to fight their way in!" Tshombe threatened. "Katanga troops will not fire first and we do not intend any aggression. But if U.N. troops try to land there, that will be an act of aggression and we will oppose it!"

Tshombe knew that once a U.N. military force had control of Katanga, the way would be open for Lumumba to end his secession and restore the province to the Republic. He fenced by wiring Hammarskjöld that he would be willing to discuss a political settlement with Bunche in Elizabethville.

Bunche promptly flew to Katanga, primarily to determine whether Tshombe's military bluster was a bluff. He reported back to Hammarskjöld that Tshombe apparently meant business. Katanga had mobilized an army of Lunda tribesmen led by Tshombe's hired white paramilitary units. Worried, Hammarskjöld postponed the U.N.'s advance into Katanga. Flying back to New York, he called a new Security Council meeting.

The news reached Lumumba in Guinea. On his way back from the U.N. he had been shopping in African capitals for military support against the Belgians. Enraged by Hammarskjöld's change of mind, he denounced the Secretary General for succumbing to "blackmail by the traitor Tshombe." He wired Gizenga to ignore Von Horn and prepare to attack Katanga independently.

Promises of military aid were given to Lumumba by Morocco, Guinea, Egypt and Ghana, where Kwame Nkrumah had assured him he would not be without help from "other countries which value . . . African independence." As though to underline that assurance, the staffs of the Soviet and Czech embassies in Leopoldville began to swell to unprecedented numbers.

A new Russian ambassador told Von Horn that the increased staffs were needed for "security reasons," because of rising unrest in the city. Militant young Congolese were staging angry demonstrations outside the Belgian Embassy and U.N. headquarters. Events suddenly took an unexpected twist.

ABAKO, Kasavubu's party, sent a cable to Hammarskjöld in New York announcing that it no longer considered Lumumba capable of stabilizing the Congo. Calling for his removal, ABAKO demanded a new, looser federal system of government with autonomous Bakongo and Katanga Provinces. Clearly, Lumumba's fragile republic was about to be shaken by fresh storms that might blow it out of existence.

At the emergency Security Council meeting summoned by Hammarskjöld on August 8, the Russians demanded that U.N. troops be authorized to shoot their way into Katanga and drive out the Belgian forces. Hammarskjöld defeated their resolution by warning that a shooting war in Katanga might rapidly escalate into a world conflict.

He asked for and won, instead, a resolution authorizing the entry of U.N. troops into Katanga for the sole purpose of ensuring withdrawal of Belgian troops, but with no involvement in the internal conflict between Lumumba and Tshombe. Gizenga, speaking for the Congo Republic, accepted the resolution. Belgium and the U.S.S.R. went along grudgingly.

But Lumumba, who had returned to Leopoldville, angrily proclaimed a state of emergency and mobilized the A.N.C. for an attack on Katanga. He dismissed ABAKO's telegram to Hammarskjöld as the work of disgruntled ABAKO jobseekers, "backed by the imperialist press" that was seeking to split Kasavubu away from him. They had failed, he insisted; he and "King Kasa" stood firmly united behind the Republic.

Kasavubu maintained an enigmatic silence.

Faced by a new double threat from both Von Horn's U.N. Army and Lumumba's unruly A.N.C. forces, Tshombe began a crafty game of stalling for time by doubletalk, equivocation, ploys and feints. U.N. troops could enter Katanga, he told Hammarskjöld, under ten conditions. First and foremost, no representative of the Central Government could accompany them.

Hammarskjöld rejected all conditions, but told Tshombe he was willing to come to Elizabethville to discuss arrangements. Tshombe quickly agreed. Unaware of these negotiations, Lumumba went ahead with his own plans. He ordered the Belgian Embassy in Leopoldville to shut down, and summoned home all Congolese students studying in Belgium. "They are being brainwashed," he charged, "for treason to the Republic!"

Washington found itself caught in a cross-fire of suspicion about American support for Hammarskjöld. Eyskens, the Belgian Premier, bitterly reminded the State Department that Brussels had originally set up its Kamina base in the Congo at NATO's insistence that it was essential for "Western defense." He announced a cut in Belgium's NATO commitments.

"I do not say Belgium will leave NATO," he told reporters curtly, "but I now fully understand that generosity does not pay!" Moscow was equally unhappy with Washington.

The United States, charged the Kremlin, was secretly supporting Belgian moves to stay in Katanga in order to keep Brussels in the anti-Communist NATO alliance. As evidence Moscow produced a copy of a letter from the State Department to the U.S. ambassador in Leopoldville. It referred to Tshombe as a "probably reliable" paid American agent, and further outraged African sentiment by musing, "God knows what these blacks will do!" Washington quickly branded the letter a Soviet forgery to discredit American foreign policy.

On August 9, 1960, Tshombe sent agents fanning through South Africa, Rhodesia and British East Africa to hire more mercenary troops with combat experience. Volunteers for his

"White Legion" were offered $300 a month and the opportunity to "fight Communism," which to most mercenaries simply meant the adventure and excitement of battle.

In Kasai, meanwhile, Kalonji appealed to Lumumba for A.N.C. troops to fight off the ferocious Bena Lulua, who were slaughtering thousands of his Baluba and burning their villages. But his cry for help went unanswered, and hundreds of thousands of terrified Baluba fled into the bush.

The disillusioned Kalonji broke with the Central Government and proclaimed South Kasai an independent Baluba "Mining State." This new secession represented a loss to the Central Government of Kasai's valuable industrial diamond mines.

Another revolt against Lumumba was signaled on August 10 when, in the African quarter of Leopoldville, an angry mob of ABAKO-Bakongo attacked him personally. Rescued by his supporters, the badly shaken Prime Minister cabled Hammarskjöld his full support of the new U.N. resolution.

He then demanded that Ralph Bunche order Von Horn to return all arms and equipment confiscated from A.N.C. forces. It was absurd, he insisted, that the legitimate Government of the Congo should be kept defenceless against insurrectionist forces. The U.N. could not stay in the Congo forever.

Bunche could not deny that Lumumba was now supporting, and Tshombe defying, the U.N. resolution. He ordered Von Horn to rearm the Congolese army.

"Have you gone mad, Ralph?" the U.N. Commander exclaimed. "Don't you realize that this will mean civil war? . . . The A.N.C. is just a rabble, not a disciplined body. As long as we keep their arms locked up they can't do much harm, but once they lay hands on them God help the civilian population—let alone our own troops!" He refused to issue the order. Bunche coldly issued it over his head.

The main force of U.N. troops now thinly controlled all provinces except Southern Kasai and Katanga. Tshombe was defending his borders with 13,000 troops, daily reinforced by new units of his White Legion. On August 12, Hammarskjöld halted the U.N. army outside Katanga while he personally led an advance guard of 220 Swedish troops into Elizabethville to negotiate with Tshombe.

In a show of reasonableness, hoping to forestall a full-scale invasion, Tshombe agreed to let U.N. troops fly in and begin taking over guard duties at Elizabethville's airport.

Lumumba was incensed because Hammarskjöld had gone to Katanga without even consulting him. He lashed out at the Secretary General for making white troops the first U.N. forces to enter Katanga, and for treating Tshombe with kid gloves. It was all part of a Western plot against him, Lumumba cried.

"Hammarskjöld and Von Horn are Swedes," he pointed out bitterly, "and everybody knows the close links between Sweden and the Belgian royal family." He demanded that *all* white troops get out of the Congo, the Belgians immediately.

Lumumba was not far off the mark in suspecting Von Horn of Belgian sympathies. The U.N. Commander tried to get Hammarskjöld to agree that it was senseless to disrupt "a well-organized state like Katanga" under a "clever, able and adroit" leader like Tshombe. But Hammarskjöld rebuked him angrily, reminding him of their U.N. mandate to expel the Belgians.

Hammarskjöld would not accede to Lumumba's demand, however, that all Tshombe's forces be disarmed and their

121

arms turned over to the A.N.C. He flew back to New York to consult the Security Council once again.

Lumumba declared martial law in the Congo, ordering A.N.C. officers to investigate all U.N. personnel suspected of being "Belgian spies." Some Canadians and other white U.N. forces were surrounded by "para [paratroop] hunters" and beaten up savagely. President Eisenhower, shocked by this Government-inspired violence, called the state of affairs "deplorable."

U.N. troops, meanwhile, began entering Katanga by air and rail, meeting almost no resistance from Tshombe's forces. At Von Horn's request, the Belgian general Gheysen agreed to withdraw all his troops to the base at Kamina by August 19, for subsequent departure to Belgium. The take-over was arranged so cordially, in fact, that Gheysen did not hesitate to offer Von Horn a little friendly military advice.

The way to handle hostile African crowds, he confided helpfully, was not just to use tear gas and riot sticks but also to throw fragmentation grenades at them.

Lumumba grew steadily more enraged by the U.N.'s handling of Katanga, and by Hammarskjöld's refusal to consult with the Central Government on U.N. strategy. His choler was inflamed by drugs and alcohol. Lines of strain now furrowed his brow, and his cheeks hollowed for lack of eating. His behavior became increasingly erratic and unpredictable.

Demanding Hammarskjöld's ouster as Secretary General by the U.N. for "treason," he threatened an alternative.

"We are easily capable of reestablishing order ourselves with our own troops," he warned, "and with the direct help of certain countries who already have pledged to help us!"

At the new meeting of the Security Council, the U.S.S.R.

pressed for a vote of no confidence against Hammarskjöld, but the move failed. A new blow to Lumumba quickly followed.

On August 22, representatives of ABAKO, M.N.C.-Kalonji and PUNA met with a CONAKAT delegation led by Tshombe. The Katangan leader made a stunning announcement: "We are determined to overthrow Lumumba. . . . He will fall within 15 days!"

Shaken, Lumumba sought to make his peace with Hammarskjöld by abruptly declaring that he was now convinced that the U.N. would get all Belgian forces out of the Congo in a week. Sending a thousand rearmed A.N.C. troops to Kasai, he ordered General Victor Lundula to capture the capital, Bakwanga; end Kalonji's "Mining State" secession; then push on south to attack Katanga and overthrow Tshombe.

Lundula's campaign against Kalonji's Baluba was less warfare than a savage bloodbath. As many as 400 Baluba men, women and children were slaughtered daily. Only 450 Baluba had modern weapons; the rest, fighting with spears, arrows and clubs, were massacred. Outraged, Hammarskjöld charged Lumumba with ordering an act of genocide.

To demonstrate African support for his regime, Lumumba called a Conference of Independent African Nations in Leopoldville on August 25. Ghana, Guinea, Ethiopia, Morocco, the United Arab Republic, Sudan, Tunisia and five other countries sent representatives. But ABAKO mounted anti-Lumumba demonstrations that turned into street riots. The delegates were shocked by the brutality of Lumumba's police.

The Soviet union sent an important mission, led by war hero Marshal George K. Zhukov, to talk to African leaders at the conference. Zhukov publicly offered Lumumba scholarships at Soviet universities for 150 Congolese students. Privately he discussed utilization of the flow of Soviet agents, planes and equipment entering the Congo.

The news worried Washington. If Lumumba survived the Congo crisis largely through Soviet help, Moscow would be welcomed as the dominant foreign presence in the Congo. That in turn would give the Russians great influence in Africa. On the other hand, if Lumumba fell and was replaced by a pro-Western Congolese, other independent African states would be convinced of a "colonial plot." They might turn to the U.S.S.R. for protection against any more "imperialist adventures."

Lumumba sought to weaken the drive against him by his political foes through diverting Congolese anger against the common enemy—the Belgians. He whipped up nationalist hysteria by encouraging mobs everywhere to engage in patriotic "para-hunting." The arrival of white U.N. units anywhere in the Congo sparked immediate rumors that they were Belgian paratroops. Millions of Congolese had never seen or known any white persons except Belgians, and were easily misled.

A flight of Russian planes was expected on August 27, and Lumumba flew to Stanleyville to greet them. Before they arrived, however, an American Globemaster flew in with Canadian U.N. signal troops. Word flashed around the city that the Belgians had landed paratroops to seize Lumumba.

A huge crowd of Congolese police, soldiers and civilians surged to the airport. The American crewmen and Canadian signalmen were savagely attacked, arrested and dragged off to jail. Some were seriously injured. They were rescued by

Ethiopian U.N. troops and flown to Leopoldville, where Von Horn had massed more troops to protect them.

"I was so mad," he recalled later, "I promised to fire the first shot myself if there was any interference."

Meanwhile, Lundula's troops in Kasai had captured Bakwanga, sending Kalonji fleeing south for refuge to Tshombe. The A.N.C. advanced to within 20 miles of Katanga's northwest border. Tshombe flew up from Elizabethville to command the defence of the province. He had mined the roads and railway bridges, he warned Lundula, and would blow them up under the A.N.C. if they dared continue their advance.

On August 30 the U.N. reported that all Belgian combat forces had left the Congo, with only some specialists left behind at the bases of Kitona and Kamina. Delegates at the African Conference in Leopoldville, impressed, passed a resolution calling for cooperation between the U.N. and the Congo Republic. Lumumba felt compelled to praise the U.N. for its work, and to promise protection for its forces.

But he still vowed his intention to "liberate our countrymen in Katanga." Defying a U.N. edict requiring all aid for the Congo to be channeled through Von Horn, he permitted 14 Ilyushin troop transport planes to supply him with a cargo of automatic rifles and 168 Soviet military experts. The planes then ferried A.N.C. reinforcements to General Lundula. Two Russian ships docked at Matadi with food, equipment, medical teams, technicians, diplomats and correspondents.

It was now clear that the Soviet Union was fully and openly supporting Lumumba. At the U.N. the Soviet delegate once more denounced Hammarskjöld's refusal to suppress the rebellious regime of Tshombe. He threw a bombshell into the Security Council by announcing that the U.S.S.R. therefore felt no obligation to pay its share of the Congo operation.

Lumumba defended his opening of the Congo to direct Soviet intervention by arguing that it was Tshombe who had first exposed the country to Cold War politics by his alliance with the Belgians. But the Western powers no longer had any illusions about Lumumba's neutrality. CIA undercover agents began working with his rivals for his overthrow.

On September 3, provided with a large force of White Legion mercenaries by Tshombe, Kalonji counterattacked A.N.C. troops holding Bakwanga. Battles raged throughout Kasai, making 300,000 Baluba refugees. Thousands who escaped slaughter died of hunger and disease. Lundula's forces were forced to fall back in heavy fighting, defeated.

From Paris, General Charles de Gaulle contemptuously castigated the "so-called United Nations" for botching its mission in the Congo. That wretched land was now like a field of haystacks into which burning torches had been flung. No sooner were flames beaten out at one point than they burst out in another. Hammarskjöld and his U.N. "firemen" fought desperately to bring the conflagration under control before it spread through Africa, and then into the nuclear skies.

Lumumba was now deeply worried. His prestige had suffered badly from his deal with the Russians and the massacre of the Baluba in Kasai. His forces had been beaten off by Kalonji, without even reaching Katanga. He was stunned on September 5 when Kasavubu suddenly went on the air at 8:15 P.M. to make a nationwide broadcast.

Denouncing Lumumba for "plunging the nation into fratricidal warfare," the President of the Republic told the Congo and the world that he was firing his Prime Minister.

# 11
# The Murder That Shook the World

HE WAS ALSO DISMISSING SIX pro-Lumumba cabinet ministers, Kasavubu proclaimed. The new Prime Minister would be Senator Joseph Ileo, former editor of *Conscience Africain*. Kasavubu called upon the U.N. to assume full responsibility for law and order under the new administration.

Stunned, Lumumba rushed to the radio station. Finding his way blocked by an armed guard, he sent Kasavubu's men sprawling with a roar of rage and stormed into the building. Commandeering a live microphone, he told the astonished Congo that *he* was firing Kasavubu as President.

"I am still in control of the country," he cried. "Remain faithful to me!" In addition to being Prime Minister, he announced, he would also serve as President.

The bewildered Senate refused to endorse the edicts of either leader, leaving the status of the Government in total confusion.

In a fight for political survival, Lumumba made several subsequent broadcasts the same night. Branding Kasavubu "an imperialist stooge," he charged: "U.N. troops are only parading in the Congo instead of aiding us!" He warned the

U.N. and the Western Powers not to interfere in a private quarrel.

Hammarskjöld and Von Horn were worried about the possibility of a major Russian airlift to Leopoldville in support of Lumumba. So, using the excuse of preventing civil war, they rushed U.N. troops to seize control of the airport. To stop any more inflammatory broadcasts, they also took over the Leopoldville radio station. Kasavubu simply crossed the Congo River to Brazzaville, where the Bakongo of the formerly French Congo let him continue to broadcast attacks on Lumumba.

Lumumba was now darkly convinced that Kasavubu was acting with the secret approval of Hammarskjöld. Why, he challenged, had the U.N. refused to involve itself in his dispute with Tshombe, yet been so quick to intervene in his conflict with Kasavubu? And why were U.N. troops blocking flights of Soviet planes to Leopoldville, while 25 Belgian planes carrying 100 tons of arms were allowed to land in Katanga?

On September 7, President Eisenhower charged that the unilateral Russian intervention in the Congo was "aggravating an already serious situation which finds Africans killing other Africans." He accused Khrushchev of being "motivated entirely by the Soviet Union's political designs in Africa."

Khrushchev attacked Hammarskjöld for favoring Katanga by "systematically violating" U.N. Security Council decisions. It was an open secret that hundreds of Belgian officers and men had been transferred to Tshombe's White Legion, along with the new planes and arms flown in from Brussels.

Hammarskjöld angrily asked the Security Council for authority to disarm A.N.C. troops and to bar Soviet military interference in the Congo. Warning that the country was on the brink of collapse, he demanded $100 million in U.N. funds for a crash program to provide jobs, open schools and operate essential government services. India's Rajeshwar Dayal was dispatched to replace Ralph Bunche as Hammarskjöld's special representative to the Congo.

Meeting separately with both Lumumba and Kasavubu, Dayal found each insisting that the other no longer had authority. Lumumba had persuaded a rump council of ministers to support him and dismiss Kasavubu for high treason. Kasavubu insisted that Ileo was now Prime Minister. Gizenga, Lumumba's deputy, appealed to Red China, which had no obligation to abide by U.N. decisions as the Soviet Union did, to rush volunteers, arms, tanks, money and food to Lumumba's aid.

"Considering the relative geographic position of the Congo and of China," Peking replied, "it is difficult to send military volunteers. However, the Government of China is placing one million pounds at the disposal of the Government of the Congo." The Congo was now clearly developing into a dangerous battleground for extending the Cold War.

At the U.N., Africa's independent nations rallied to Lumumba's cause over the sensitive issue of colonialism.

"Let me assure you that Tshombes do not exist in Mali," Mali's representative told the Security Council. The Guinea delegate demanded the return of Guinea troops from the U.N. force, which he accused of trying to "break up Africa to the satisfaction of the colonial powers." He added, "Guinea could well be the Congo, and the Congo, Africa."

The Moroccan delegate declared, "We cannot be passive spectators to the rebirth of colonialism and its return to the

Congo." In the eyes of his anticolonial neighbors, Lumumba was a "black Messiah" and a "Lincoln of the Congo."

Chaos in the Congo deepened when the A.N.C. army, unpaid for two months, threatened a new revolt, this time to seize power. On September 10 the A.N.C. Chief of Staff, 31-year-old Colonel Joseph Mobutu, received money rushed to him by the U.N. and presided over a pay parade.

Next day rival Congo delegations left for the U.N. One represented Lumumba, the other Kasavubu; each claimed to be the official delegation. From Ghana, Nkrumah appealed for a reconciliation of the feuding leaders.

"You cannot afford, my brother, to be harsh and uncompromising," he urged Lumumba. "Do not force Kasavubu out now. It will bring too much trouble in Leopoldville. Be as cool as a cucumber. Patrice, if you fail, it will be due to your unwillingness to face the facts of life."

The Republic was now paralyzed between the locked forces of President and Prime Minister. In a sudden surprise move, Colonel Mobutu seized power from both rivals. A devout Catholic alienated by Lumumba's negotiations with the Soviet Union, he announced that as head of the A.N.C. army he was taking over the Government because of the incompetence of the politicians.

"This is a truce," he declared, "not a revolution."

General Von Horn, who had sealed off the government radio station, now reopened it for Mobutu. Appealing for calm, the new strong man promised that the military regime would only last three months, during which time technicians would be called in to run the country and rescue it from anarchy.

The Congo seethed with new excitement. Kasavubu remained in seclusion at his Stanley Falls residence. Lumumba sought to locate Mobutu and remonstrate with him. The ousted Prime Minister suspected a CIA plot behind the coup d'etat; he knew that CIA agents were now flooding into the Congo in great numbers to counterbalance Soviet agents.

Unable to locate Mobutu at Camp Leopold, Lumumba made the mistake of staying there overnight. His presence infuriated hundreds of Baluba troops, who blamed him for the atrocities against their fellow tribesmen in Kasai.

Actually, Tshombe's forces were equally to blame, beating, raping, mutilating and massacring Baluba for supporting Sendwe's anti-Tshombe BALUBAKAT Party. Crazed Baluba survivors were reverting to savagery and cannibalism as they swept through Kasai in raids for food and revenge.

At Camp Leopold, enraged A.N.C. Baluba troops sought to mob and kill Lumumba. He was rescued by Ghanian U.N. troops, who were then assigned to guard his official residence. Wan and shaken, Lumumba sensed that time was running out on him.

At the U.N. the Security Council beat off an attempt by the Soviet Union to discredit and replace Hammarskjöld and Von Horn, both of whom now had the full support of the United States and most independent African nations. Even radical states like Ghana and Guinea were reluctant to weaken the U.N., which they recognized as an indispensable protector of smaller against greater powers.

Mobutu gave Russian and Czech diplomats in Leopoldville 48 hours to leave the country. He also put A.N.C. troops in an outer ring around the Ghanian U.N. troops surrounding Lumumba's residence. There was immediate speculation that

Lumumba was under house arrest, and that Kasavubu had the army's favor.

On September 16, Mobutu threw a guard around the Parliament building and sealed it off. Kasavubu, still regarded as President, then dutifully announced that he was dismissing the Parliament, and that a military regime headed by Mobutu would temporarily run the Government.

Thirty of Lumumba's chief aides were seized and jailed. Lumumba himself would not be arrested, Mobutu announced, as long as he caused no trouble. Gizenga, Lumumba's Deputy Premier, had fled to Stanleyville, where he was organizing Oriental Province against Mobutu. He was joined by General Victor Lundula, who had been stripped of control of the A.N.C. army by Mobutu's pay parade. Together they purged Stanleyville of all Mobutu supporters, cut all ties to Leopoldville and prepared to hold the province for Lumumba.

Mobutu set up a "College of High Commissioners," headed by Justin Bomboko and university graduate students, to run the country until the end of the year. The students were willing enough, but found the country's affairs in such a shambles that they didn't know what to do first or how to do it.

Bomboko asked Belgian instructors at the university to aid them. The instructors in turn asked former Belgian officials to return and help. To the astonishment of the Congolese, it seemed as though the Belgians were returning in full strength to take over the Congo once more.

To add to the confusion, the new strong man of the Congo found his control over his troops slipping. The A.N.C. was once more behaving brutally toward civilians, black and white alike, as well as looting and deserting. Without consulting Mobutu, the new student commissioners asked the

132

U.N. to take over patrolling duties from the A.N.C. Outraged, Mobutu arrested Bomboko.

Leopoldville now fell into a fresh uproar—students against Mobutu, Mobutu against the college, U.N. forces against the A.N.C., returned Belgians against the U.N.

Lumumba denounced Mobutu's actions as illegal and inspired by "certain powers," and he vowed to bring back the Russian and Czech diplomats Mobutu had expelled. He was still the Prime Minister, he insisted, claiming he had reached a reconciliation and new understanding with Kasavubu.

That, Kasavubu commented acidly, was news to him.

Mobutu angrily demanded that Dayal remove the U.N. guard around Lumumba's residence to permit his arrest. Dayal refused and reported to Hammarskjöld at the U.N. that Mobutu and his youthful College of Commissioners had lost control of the A.N.C., which was once more as undisciplined as ever.

Dayal blamed the Belgians for the clashes between U.N. forces and government troops. The best hope of restoring peace to the Congo now, he advised, lay in a settlement between Lumumba and his political rivals.

Dayal's report brought an Afro-Asian resolution on the floor of the U.N. General Assembly. It called upon all nations to refrain from unilateral aid to any Congo faction. Expressing confidence in Hammarskjöld's policies, it also insisted that he get all Belgian forces out of the Congo at once.

The resolution passed unanimously.

Kasavubu flew to the U.N. to lead the fight for recognition of his delegation. His credentials from Mobutu, the de facto power in the Congo, persuaded the General Assembly to seat his delegation in place of Lumumba's. Jubilant, "King Kasa"

133

flew home on November 27 to a victory celebration in Leopoldville arranged for him by Mobutu.

Until then Lumumba had continued to nurture hopes of a reconciliation with Kasavubu. He now realized that his only hope of regaining power was to take a leaf from Tshombe's notebook and develop his own rival state, in Oriental Province. That night he fled to Leopoldville in a closed car.

The U.N. guard, under orders only to protect his residence, made no attempt to prevent his departure. In the confusion of the celebration for Kasavubu, Lumumba's car sped unchallenged through the outer ring of government troops.

Heading for Stanleyville, four days' drive distant, he felt so secure that he didn't bother to cover his tracks. At several small villages en route he made fiery speeches attacking the Leopoldville "traitors." The news spread.

Mobutu's troops sped after him in hot pursuit. Catching up with him at Port Francqui (Kasai), they beat him savagely in the act of taking him prisoner. The Ghanaian U.N. commander in Kasai wired Dayal for permission to rescue him. Dayal sped the request to New York, but the reply was negative. The U.N. could not interfere in internal affairs.

General Von Horn was frankly relieved.

"To put it bluntly," he declared, "had Lumumba got to Stanleyville, the whole Congo might have gone up in flames."

Two days after his arrest, Lumumba was brought back to Leopoldville in a battered condition. A U.N. report described his condition upon arrival: "without his glasses and with a soiled shirt; his hair was in disorder, he had a blood clot on his cheek, and his hands were tied behind his back."

Next day, head shaven to humiliate him, he was flown to Thysville for imprisonment in Camp Hardy. Dayal protested indignantly to Kasavubu, who coolly reminded him that the U.N. itself had accused Lumumba of genocide against the Baluba in Kasai. But most Afro-Asian states were angrily demanding to know why the U.N. Command in Leopoldville was taking steps to prevent a popular uprising for Lumumba's rescue.

Oriental Province went into open revolt. General Lundula, supplied by Egypt's Nasser with funds to pay Stanleyville troops and keep them loyal to Lumumba, called for an attack on Leopoldville. On December 9, Gizenga threatened to arrest and perhaps execute all Belgians in Oriental Province unless Mobutu and Kasavubu released Lumumba.

Three days later he proclaimed Stanleyville the legitimate capital of the Congo Republic. The Lumumbaist forces, he insisted, controlled far more of the country than the Leopold-ville regime. He accused Mobutu of holding power only by virtue of American money and supplies. Gizenga's regime was promptly recognized by the Communist bloc powers. Through the Russian and Czech embassies, now established in Stanleyville, he received arms, supplies and funds.

By Christmas, 1960, Lundula's forces had overrun Kivu and northern Katanga, reducing Mobutu's area of control to Leopoldville and Equator Provinces and parts of Kasai. The U.N.'s tiny forces in Kivu were helpless to stop outrages committed by A.N.C. troops against Belgian missionaries and nuns.

Freed of all restraints, marijuana-smoking government soldiers burned native villages, outraged women and destroyed gardens and livestock. Their atrocities reflected less on Lumumba, in whose name they ran amok, than on the Mobutu-Kasavubu regime for its inability to keep order. To add to the chaos, Tshombe was persecuting the hapless Baluba in Katanga, to crush BALUBAKAT opposition to CONAKAT.

Kasavubu sought to blame Rajeshwar Dayal for the turmoil, and demanded his recall as head of U.N. operations in the Congo. But a conference of Afro-Asian powers at Casablanca demanded that Mobutu's "lawless bands" be disarmed and Lumumba restored as Prime Minister. Hoping to work out some plan of conciliation, Kasavubu summoned all province leaders to a conference. Gizenga and Tshombe refused to attend.

In the United States, meanwhile, a new president took office. Studying the Congo situation, John F. Kennedy was convinced that it was fraught with danger for world peace by the polarization of the U.S. and the U.S.S.R. on opposite sides. He let it be known that he favored the restoration of Lumumba as the best hope of stabilizing the Congo.

Worried, Kasavubu and Mobutu decided to transfer Lumumba to a secret place of detention from which it would be impossible for his followers or U.N. forces to rescue him. On January 17, 1961, he was flown to an undisclosed destination with two of his aides. Apparently the plan was to imprison them at Bakwanga, where other arrested Lumumba officials had been "tried" and executed by the Baluba for the A.N.C. massacres in Kasai. But finding the U.N. in control of the airport, the pilot bypassed Bakwanga and flew on to Elizabethville.

Roped together, the three prisoners were manhandled sadistically by their guards all through the flight. "They were so severely beaten up," the pilot later testified, "that the Belgian crew was disgusted, and shut themselves up in the front cabin." Lumumba and his aides could barely stagger off the plane at Elizabethville. They were then compelled to run a gauntlet between lines of Tshombe's solders and police, who beat them with clubs.

Tshombe later admitted to a U.N. commission that he had seen the three prisoners that night, and that they were in bad shape. Lumumba, "whose face was all puffed up," had appealed to him for protection. But two days later Tshombe announced that, by Kasavubu's request, he was holding "the traitor Patrice Lumumba" prisoner in Katanga because "the prison at Thysville no longer offers sufficient guarantees."

Word of the arrest and mistreatment of Lumumba flashed through the Congo, provoking an uproar. Kasavubu and Mobutu grew alarmed as crowds surged through the streets of Leopoldville shouting furious demands for Lumumba's release and return. Mobutu found himself unable to control even the A.N.C. troops directly under his command.

The new anarchy in the Congo caused the despairing U.N. Security Council to consider suspending its independence and operating it as a U.N. protectorate. Kasavubu quickly warned that he would tolerate no such move. He replaced Mobutu's ineffective College of Commissioners with a new cabinet under Joseph Ileo as Prime Minister.

Conferring with Mobutu and Tshombe, he agreed with them that no leader of the Republic or a province could feel secure in his power as long as Lumumba remained a storm center of opposition from jail. Revolts would break out continually, in the name of freeing him from martyrdom. Like Kenyatta in Kenya, his imprisonment would keep the country in turmoil until he was released and elevated to power. Only his death could eliminate that possibility.

In Elizabethville, Lumumba and his two fellow prisoners were turned over to the custody of Tshombe's Minister of the Interior, Godefroid Munongo, described by General Von Horn as "a man drenched and impregnated in evil." Munongo, grandson of the sadistic Bayeke king M'Siri, had served the Belgian colonial administration as a local police court judge. During Tshombe's frequent travels out of Katanga, Munongo was left in charge of the CONAKAT Government.

Munongo ordered the prisoners taken to a farmhouse outside Elizabethville. Circumstantial evidence of what happened next was pieced together by a subsequent U.N. investigation. On February 10, Munongo brought Tshombe and another Katanga cabinet minister to the farmhouse.

They watched two Belgian mercenaries, under orders from Munongo, brutalize and murder Patrice Lumumba. There was some testimony later that Munongo himself had also plunged a bayonet into Lumumba's chest. Lumumba's two aides were also killed, primarily to silence them as witnesses.

Two days later Munongo went on the Elizabethville radio station to report that Lumumba and his aides had escaped from the farmhouse, and gave the details. A car they had stolen ran out of gas and had been found overturned in a ditch. Katanga Government had offered an $8,000 bounty for their recapture. All three men had been traced and "massacred by the inhabitants of a small village." The villagers "may have acted somewhat precipitously, though excusably," but would collect the reward. Munongo refused to name the village or gravesite for fear of "eventual reprisals" by Lumumbaists.

"I will speak frankly," he concluded cynically. "If people accuse us of killing Lumumba, I will reply: 'Prove it!'"

The news rocked the Congo and stunned the world.

No one believed Munongo's story; it was taken for granted that Lumumba had been murdered on the orders of Tshombe as a Belgian stooge. Most Africans saw the assassination as a decision by white colonialists to eliminate the most dangerous black nationalist in the Congo.

London papers carried black headlines: COMMONS IN UPROAR OVER MURDER OF MR. LUMUMBA. In New York they announced: FIGHTING AT U.N. OVER LUMUMBA. 'MURDER' CRIES BY BRAWLING NEGROES. Afro-Asian governments expressed outrage at the U.N. for permitting Lumumba's arrest and execution.

Khrushchev, renaming a Soviet university after Lumumba, demanded the punishment of all "imperialist powers" responsible for his death. Furious anti-Belgian demonstrations raged in 30 cities around the world. In Cairo the Belgian Embassy was sacked and burned by mobs.

Overnight Lumumba had become a symbol of African martyrdom to white colonialism. How could the Central Government of the Congo, which had cooperated in arranging his murder, now survive the wrath of its outraged people?

# 12
# A Plane Disappears

LUMUMBA'S WIFE WALKED THROUGH Leopoldville naked to the waist, an ancient tribal rite of mourning. The sight of her stirred Lumumba's supporters to enraged street riots against Kasavubu's Bakongo followers. Kasavubu struck back by transferring six leading Lumumbaists from jail in Thysville to Bakwanga, for "trial" and execution by Kalonji's Baluba.

Gizenga retaliated by machine-gunning the Mobutu adherents he was holding in Stanleyville jails.

On February 15, Red China, the Soviet Union, Ghana, Guinea, the U.A.R., Morocco, Algeria and Mali recognized the Gizenga regime in Stanleyville as the only "lawful government" of the Congo. Joined by Libya, India, Indonesia, Ceylon and Yugoslavia, they petitioned Hammarskjöld for an immediate investigation of Lumumba's murder.

"I couldn't give a damn," Tshombe growled. "If others will leave us alone we will solve our problems. Both East and West must keep their noses out of our affairs."

Munongo blustered, "I forbid the United Nations to take a position in this matter!" Kasavubu, hoping to keep the lightning diverted to Katanga to obscure his own blame for putting

Lumumba in Tshombe's hands, piously called upon Parliament for a minute of silent tribute to "a sincere patriot who got involved with bad foreigners."

Lumumba had made serious mistakes as the first African leader to wield power in the Republic, but none as unwise as the decision of his political enemies to kill him brutally. He had called for Communist assistance, but only after the leading Western powers of the U.N. had refused to allow him to unify the Congo by ending Tshombe's secession.

"One wonders," speculated an American TV news commentator, "whether Lincoln, too, might not have accepted Russian help to save our Union, if Western Europe had intervened in the Civil War to prevent him from sending Government troops to the South to put down secession."

Lumumba's abrasive and domineering personality had certainly not been helpful in unifying the Congo. His inflexible zeal had made him insist that centuries-old tribal traditions be replaced overnight by patriotism to a brand-new republic. Instead of conciliating leaders like Kasavubu and Tshombe, skillfully accommodating their egos and tribal ties, he had united them against him by his arrogance.

But perhaps no leader could have prevented a Congo unprepared for independence from falling into anarchy.

With Lumumba out of the way, Kasavubu moved swiftly to consolidate his power and prevent U.N. forces from disarming government troops and putting the Congo under a guardianship. Mobutu stepped aside, and once more a new government was formed with Ileo as Prime Minister. Kasavubu invited Tshombe to become Ileo's deputy. Gizenga and Kalonji were also offered cabinet portfolios. All three were promised constitutional revisions to give greater powers to the provinces.

On February 14, 1961, the Soviet Union launched a new attack at the U.N. against Hammarskjöld. Accusing him as an "accomplice" in the murder of Lumumba, the Russians demanded the withdrawal of all U.N. forces from the Congo.

Suspecting a Soviet plan to supply new military aid to Gizenga as Lumumba's heir, President Kennedy warned that the United States would oppose the attempt by any power to intervene in the Congo unilaterally. A week later the U.N. Security Council passed a new resolution authorizing the U.N. army in the Congo to use whatever force was necessary to prevent civil war. Copies were sent to all Congo leaders.

Ileo denounced it as a violation of Congolese sovereignty. Tshombe and Kalonji flew to Elizabethville at his invitation. The three leaders agreed to cooperate in fighting both U.N. "tutelage" and "Communist tyranny" without outside help.

On March 8 they called a conference of all province leaders at Tananarive, Madagascar. Gizenga was invited, but warily refused to attend. Tshombe, as the most powerful political figure present, won approval for his plan to reorganize the Congo into a "Community of Congolese States," a loose confederation with new province boundaries drawn along tribal lines. Its net effect would be to carve the Congo into a patchwork of tiny, relatively powerless states, of which Katanga would be the largest and strongest.

"We have resolved our problems ourselves," Tshombe declared in delight, "and now we want both West and East to leave us alone." Even as he spoke his White Legion mercenaries were blazing their way into villages of northern Katanga and Kivu, driving out and massacring anti-Tshombe Baluba and controlling their territory for Katanga.

In a March interview with a *New York Times* reporter, Tshombe denied that he was a Belgian puppet or front man for Union Miniere. "I have no inferiority complex toward the white man as do some of my Congolese colleagues," he added. But he frankly admitted his dependence on whites for control: "I have the only disciplined army in the Congo today and the only effective administration. Why? Because I have foreign experts. Without foreigners, Katanga would collapse into chaos."

The Tananarive Conference decision was denounced as illegal by the radical Afro-Asian block of the U.N., because Gizenga had not participated. Tshombe was charged with having engineered it to undermine U.N. support for a unified Congo.

On April 3, Tshombe sent Belgian-led mercenaries to retake the Elizabethville airport from U.N. forces holding it. His mercenaries were overpowered and arrested. Tshombe immediately mobilized Katanga for war against the U.N. He inflamed a crowd of 6,000 Africans into trying to massacre the U.N. troops at the airport.

The U.N. Command quickly flew in Irish and Indian reinforcements, who beat off the attackers, demonstrating that even in Katanga Tshombe's authority was limited. U.N. troops also clashed with the White Legion who were prosecuting Tshombe's tribal war against the Baluba. Tshombe froze all U.N. funds in Katanga banks, cut communications between U.N. units, mined roads they needed, blocked their access to and from the airport and withheld aviation gas from their planes.

143

Armed with the new U.N. resolution, Hammarskjöld was under heavy pressure from the Russians to order an all-out military attack on Katanga. But he preferred to make every effort first to bring Tshombe to terms without firing an unnecessary shot. There had been enough bloodshed in the Congo.

In a show of strength he flew 1,500 new troops a day into Elizabethville until almost half the U.N. Army was concentrated in Katanga. Hammarskjöld did not underestimate Tshombe's defiant cunning, but counted on his being held on a tight leash by Union Miniere. With world opinion behind Hammarskjöld, and the Russian block straining for Tshombe's overthrow, the realistic Belgians could have no illusions about winning a military decision over the U.N.

The enraged Tshombe was forced to limit his strategy to a combination of skirmishes, threats, promises, persuasion, denunciations, lies and deception.

At a Coquilhatville (Equator Province) Conference in April, Kasavubu told 280 Congolese leaders that the Central Government had reached an understanding with the U.N. and urged their support. Tshombe was outraged. Shrilly accusing Kasavubu of cringing before Hammarskjöld, he fell on his knees in a mocking demonstration of "King Kasa's" servility to the U.N. But the conference gave Kasavubu a vote of confidence, and approved his proposal to recall Parliament in order to elect a new government.

Tshombe stalked out of the conference in a fury. Kasavubu promptly accused him of high treason to the Republic. The conference roared a demand for Tshombe's arrest. Before his plane could leave Coquilhatville he was seized, but Ileo promised to win his release if he returned to the conference.

"If that is how you run the Congo," Tshombe grated, "you can have it!" He was held for trial on charges of assassinating Lumumba, massacring the Baluba, conspiring with Belgium and counterfeiting (printing Katangan currency).

'We are going to do everything in our power to liberate Katanga," vowed one of Kasavubu's ministers. "By force if necessary!" It was clear to Tshombe that Kasavubu had made a deal with Hammarskjöld, isolating Katanga in exchange for U.N. support of the new Central Government.

Tshombe was imprisoned for two months in Leopoldville.

Munongo carried on Katanga's resistance. He flooded the province with posters: "Tshombe suffers for you—be worthy of him!" If the U.N. tried to overthrow the CONAKAT regime, Munongo warned, he would press buttons that would destroy Katanga's vital mines and dams. He demanded Tshombe's release as the price of a settlement. If Tshombe were executed, Munongo knew, it would only be a matter of time before his own neck would be forfeit. But Tshombe was even more tender of his own skin than his deputy.

On June 22 he obtained his release by agreeing to send representatives to the new Parliament, and to place his military forces under the Congolese Army. "I will work with my Congolese brothers," he swore piously, "to make a very great country." Ten seconds after his return to Elizabethville, he expelled all A.N.C. army officers and went on the air to vow that Katanga would always remain independent.

His promises in Leopoldville were invalid, he announced blandly, because they had all been made under duress. He described his imprisonment succinctly: "It was hell!"

Seeking new ways to survive politically, he even offered to cooperate with the Soviet Union and Ghana in defying the

U.N. But the Communist block nations were committed to support Gizenga, and ignored his feeler contemptuously.

Tshombe then flew to Brazzaville in the formerly French Congo and appealed to Kasavubu across the Congo River for a reconciliation, offering to share Katanga's wealth with the Central Government. But Kasavubu was tired of Tshombe's wiles and refused to see him. Returning to Elizabethville, Tshombe frantically sought to beef up his White Legion forces by recruiting thousands of new mercenaries from South Africa. He also solicited former Algerian Foreign Legionnaires known as "the terrible ones," offering fat bonuses.

When the new Congo Parliament convened in Leopoldville, Gizenga agreed to send representatives. He and Kasavubu compromised on a neutral candidate for Prime Minister— Cyrille Adoula, a socialist labor leader. Gizenga agreed to serve as Adoula's deputy when a member of his own party, Joseph Kasongo, was named the new President of the Congo.

Gizenga's support of the new Adoula regime, which now also included adherents of Lumumba, Kasavubu, Kalonji and Sendwe, won recognition for it from the Communist block nations. Only Red China continued to insist that Gizenga's Stanleyville regime was the sole legal government in the Congo.

Adoula wrote to the U.N. urging Hammarskjöld to fly to Leopoldville at once to discuss a joint program for ending Katanga's secession. The French and British opposed a military drive to overthrow Tshombe, but Washington—for once —agreed with the Soviet Union that it was essential if the Congo was ever to succeed as a republic.

Union Miniere, stunned by these developments, now prudently began withholding support from Tshombe.

146

"You will pay dearly for your treason!" he shouted at company officials. "Remember that I have the power to seize your company and operate it as a state utility!"

The Congo, meanwhile, was still in turmoil. Tribal warfare, marked with savagery and cannibalism, raged uncontrolled through the bush country. Economic production and exports were only 25 per cent of normal. Seven out of ten Congolese were jobless, while inflation had sent prices soaring by 20 per cent. Thousands of Baluba in Kasai were starving. Only Katanga's wealth could save the rest of the Congo.

"Nothing will keep the Congolese people from recovering their heritage!" vowed Prime Minister Adoula.

In August, Conor Cruise O'Brien, now the U.N.'s special representative in Katanga, was ordered to get the mercenaries out of the province. Tshombe flatly rejected the edict.

Conferring with the chief of the U.N.'s Tunisian forces, O'Brien was told by Mahmoud Khiaria that Hammarskjöld had ordered the first sign of defiance by Tshombe to be met by seizure of Katanga's public buildings, deportation of all white officials and the arrest of Tshombe and Munongo.

As the first U.N. armored troops rolled into Elizabethville, Tshombe quickly sent word to O'Brien that he had changed his mind and was firing all his mercenaries. O'Brien held up the advance. But Tshombe was only buying time for last-minute reinforcements. His troops secretly distributed arms to the populace, and then the fighting broke out.

By the third day of the battle the U.N. forces had suffered seven dead and 26 wounded. But Katangan losses were severe —200 dead, 500 wounded. Tshombe broadcast fierce appeals for "total war" against the U.N., urging his Lunda tribesmen to fight beside the mercenaries to the last man and bullet.

But with rifles in their hands and war fever flaming, the Lunda preferred to turn their hate on their traditional tribal enemies. Thousands of Baluba were slaughtered in the African quarter of Elizabethville. Over 20,000 Baluba fled to the U.N. camp for protection and shelter.

Thousands died of starvation because the U.N. had no provisions for them. Those who returned in desperation to Elizabethville were met by murderous fire from Katangan gendarmes and white civilians. Raving Baluba began attacking whites with knives, spears and bicycle chains.

His own fief plunged into chaos, Tshombe bitterly offered to meet with Hammarskjöld in Northern Rhodesia to discuss terms for a cease-fire. Hammarskjöld was under intense pressure from Britain, France and Belgium to halt U.N. military operations before the whole Congo exploded. Agreeing to meet Tshombe at Ndola, south of Katanga, he flew off for the rendezvous on September 18.

At ten minutes past midnight his chartered Swedish DC-6B circled over Ndola airport. Suddenly the radio went dead. There was no reply to the control tower's request for identification. The plane then inexplicably disappeared.

The early morning hours brought reports of a plane crash. The U.N. scoured the surrounding countryside with search planes. At 3 P.M. on September 19 the missing plane was spotted. It had crashed and burned in a grove six miles from Ndola.

Hammarskjöld and all aboard were dead.

The disaster brought sorrowful tributes to him from the world's leaders and the dean of American journalists.

"I think what he did, and was trying to do when he died," said Walter Lippman, "will be remembered . . . because in that lies the attempt which may fail in the Congo but which will be revived in some other way, some other place—to impose conciliation and peace in a situation which might lead to the most dreadful catastrophe of war."

The day after Hammarskjöld's death, Tshombe signed a cease-fire agreement with the U.N. The truce angered Adoula, who saw in it only another vacillation by the U.N. that would permit Tshombe to avoid submitting to the Republic. The Central Government, Adoula warned on September 22, would use "its own means to put an end to the secession of Katanga." Mobutu broadcast an appeal to all black troops in Katanga to revolt against their white officers.

Tshombe urged Adoula to meet him on neutral ground to negotiate a settlement. Adoula replied coldly that Tshombe was free to come to Leopoldville for talks. But Tshombe, who had already enjoyed two months' hospitality in a Leopoldville jail, warily declined the invitation.

Mobutu led 5,000 A.N.C. troops into Katanga. Tshombe's mercenary pilots launched air strikes against the Government's forward supply depots. Suffering heavy losses of men and equipment, enraged A.N.C. units went berserk. They arrested 400 whites, beat up missionaries and assaulted women.

In Kivu Province, A.N.C. troops seized 13 Italian U.N. airmen. Accusing them of being Belgian mercenaries, Mobutu's troops beat, shot and mutilated all 13. In a desperate effort to restore control over his undisciplined "mobs in uniform," Mobutu arrested 123 of his troops and sent them back to Leopoldville under guard to await court-martial.

When the U.N. Security Council met in November, 1961, its members were gloomy over Lumumba's murder, Hammarskjöld's death, the inconclusive fighting and flagrant violations of the Katanga cease-fire agreement by Tshombe's gendarmerie.

Brushing aside British and French objections, the council authorized the new Secretary General, U Thant of Burma, "to take vigorous action, including the use of force, if necessary," to arrest and deport "all foreign military and hostile elements" in the Congo. The United States solidly supported the resolution, which put the U.N. forces squarely behind those of the Central Government.

"It is intolerable," U Thant declared, "that efforts to prevent civil war and achieve reconciliation in the Congo should be persistently obstructed and thwarted by professional adventurers who fight and kill for money."

Tshombe knew now that he was fighting for his political survival, and perhaps for his very life.

"Tomorrow or the day after there will be a trial of strength," he told a crowd of 7,000 Katangans in Elizabethville. "Let us prepare for it. Let Katangan fighters arise at the given moment in every street, every lane, every road and every village. I will give you the signal. . . . You will not be able to have guns and automatic weapons, but we still have our poisoned arrows, our spears, our axes."

Flying to Brazzaville, however, he sent hopeful messages across the river urging Adoula to join him for negotiations. Adoula refused, convinced that joint action by the Central Government and U.N. forces finally had Tshombe on the run. The desperate Katanga Premier flew to Paris to seek foreign aid there, while in New York a Belgian-financed lobby called the American Committee for Aid to Katanga Freedom Fighters agitated for American support for Tshombe.

Katanga was labeled "the Hungary of 1961," referring to the 1956 invasion of Hungary by Soviet troops to put down an anti-Soviet uprising. The lobby had the support of U.S. Senator Thomas J. Dodd of Connecticut, who had been Tshombe's guest in Elizabethville during an inspection visit.

"Tshombe is one of the most impressive men I have ever met," Dodd vowed, "and one of the most maligned men in history." But Africans, noted historian Arthur Schlesinger, had a less complimentary view of the Katangan leader as "the white colonists' black man."

In Tshombe's absence, Munongo continued violating the cease-fire agreement. U.N. leaders in Elizabethville were arrested and savagely beaten. Roadblocks cut off U.N. forces from all supplies and communications. A company of commandos in three armored cars attacked the U.N.-held airport.

U.N. Ghurka troops counterattacked swiftly on December 5, killing 38 of the commandos. Fifteen U.N. jets, flying into Katanga from Kasai, attacked bridges, hit the railway, strafed trucks and smashed Tshombe's planes on the ground.

"The United Nations may take our cities," cried Munongo. "There will remain our villages and the bush. All the tribal chiefs are alerted. We are savages; we are Negroes. So be it. We shall fight like savages with our arrows!"

# 13

# "Watch Out for These Whites!"

TEN DAYS LATER THE U.N. WAS in full control of Elizabethville. Whole streets were filled with rubble, smashed cars and
felled palm trees. Almost two-thirds of the white population
had fled.

"The United Nations died in Katanga!" Tshombe cried.

He sent a plea to President Kennedy to help arrange a
new cease-fire. Kennedy appointed Edmund Gullion the new
U.S. Ambassador to the Congo, instructing him to work out
a settlement that would end the civil war by compelling
Tshombe to accept the authority of the Central Government.

On December 21, after 17 hours of almost continuous
argument with Gullion and Adoula at Kitona, near Leopoldville, a weary Tshombe finally signed an agreement ending
Katanga's secession. He recognized Kasavubu as President
of the Congo, agreed to abide by the U.N. Security Council
resolutions and consented to put his gendarmerie under the
control of the Central Government. His only stipulation was
that his agreement would first have to be ratified by his Cabinet and the Katangan legislature.

Gullion, speaking for the United States, and Ralph Bunche,

speaking for the U.N., made it plain that unless the settlement was ratified, Tshombe would be overthrown.

But even as he flew home Tshombe was devising schemes to delay and postpone ratification of the Kitona Agreement until he could twist out of it. He counted on time as his ally. Adoula's control of the Congo was still precarious; the maddened Baluba were still rioting, pillaging and looting; Lumumbaist resistance was still strong in many areas; Gizenga's loyalty to Adoula's regime was dubious; and there was strong pressure at the U.N. to end the costly Congo intervention.

Back in Elizabethville, he told a cheering crowd, "I signed nothing in Leopoldville. . . . Our rights and cause have been defended!"

When Adoula sent a thousand A.N.C. soldiers to join U.N. troops in northern Katanga, Tshombe accused this force of committing atrocities. In sending Government troops, Tshombe also charged, Adoula had violated the Kitona Agreement, which the Katanga legislature had not yet had "time" to ratify.

Assistant U.S. Secretary of State G. Mennen Williams, speaking in Detroit, scoffed at Tshombe's "horrendous tales of indiscriminate mayhem by United Nations troops." In Philadelphia Carl T. Rowan, Deputy Assistant Secretary of State for Public Affairs, accused Tshombe of conducting a "clever big-money campaign" to peddle a "string of myths," hoping to swing American support behind him. Rowan castigated Union Miniere for having donated $140,000 to the Belgian publicity lobby beating the drums for Tshombe in New York.

Tshombe was not the only thorn in the side of Adoula.

Although Gizenga had agreed to become Deputy Premier in a new coalition government, he returned to Stanleyville and refused to take up his post in Leopoldville. Adoula, charged Gizenga, had sabotaged the original decision of Lumumba's Central Government to accept Soviet aid against Tshombe.

On Adoula's orders, Gizenga was seized and jailed for "leading a secessionist movement." When Kalonji, as well, showed signs of defecting from the coalition, he also was jailed. Followers of both leaders staged stormy protests.

Support for the Adoula regime began to wobble.

Tshombe, meanwhile, continued to accuse drug-dazed and drunken A.N.C. troops of burning, looting and murdering in northern Katanga, without any restraint from U.N. forces. He specifically charged eight A.N.C. soldiers with having massacred 22 white missionaries at Kongolo on January 23, 1962. The eight were arrested by Lundula's forces and court-martialed.

Tshombe asked the American Consul for a visa to visit the United States and make personal appeals for support. He was told that he did not have a "valid passport." One could be his, however, by ratifying the Kitona Agreement, which would make him a bona fide citizen of the Congo Republic.

Tshombe continued to stall. He asked for a one-month delay in ratification in order to get all his mercenaries safely out of Katanga. Adoula now began to realize that Tshombe had no intention of keeping his word. If that genius of procrastination could squirm out of the Kitona Agreement, Adoula's own regime would fall as incompetent.

On February 2, Adoula flew to New York to appeal to the U.N. General Assembly for all-out military aid to crush Tshombe's secession immediately and totally. Lunching with

President Kennedy, Adoula was promised that his Government would receive all necessary aid and support. But by March the elusive Tshombe was still firmly in control of Katanga.

He now had a new pretext for rejecting the Kitona Agreement. Look what had happened to Gizenga and Kalonji after they had agreed to cooperate with Adoula's regime. Once Tshombe agreed to enter Adoula's Cabinet, what was to stop Adoula from jailing him, too, if he were rash enough to disagree with any of Adoula's policies?

Nevertheless, to buy more time while he secretly secured more arms and mercenaries, Tshombe agreed to come to Leopoldville for new talks with Adoula, after the U.N. guaranteed him safe conduct. Manifesting an air of thoughtful sincerity, Tshombe dragged the talks through April 1, when they were interrupted by a nationwide two-day strike.

The Union of Congolese Workers, largest in the Republic, protested against the outrageous salaries politicians in Adoula's government had voted themselves, while unemployment was as high as 50 per cent in most urban areas. Government ministers were paid $500 a week, plus $75 weekly expenses, while the best-paid Congolese workers earned only $11 a week.

Banning all public meetings, Adoula called on the army to end the strike by jailing hundreds of union workers. Turbulence in Leopoldville turned into riots, to the unmitigated delight of Moise Tshombe. Adoula was forced to fire over half of his Cabinet. Many ministers, fearing jail, fled. Christopher Gbenye, former aide of both Lumumba and Gizenga, was arrested but freed by a vote of Parliament.

Many Congolese political leaders now dreaded Adoula as

more of a dictator than Lumumba had ever tried to be. By September former officials who had fled the country gathered in Morocco to form a Congo government in exile. They claimed to represent the M.N.C. (Lumumba's party), Gizenga's A.S.P. and Sendwe's BALUBAKAT, and were encouraged by Soviet interest. Moscow's support for Adoula and the U.N. had soured.

The United States had made a diplomatic blunder by insisting that the Russians pay their assessed share of the U.N. operation in the Congo. The Russians argued that they weren't required to pay, since the Soviet Embassy had been shut down by the Central Government without even U.N. protest.

The argument went to the World Court, which upheld the American position as legally valid. But the Russians, confident that they could depend upon a U.N. vote to sustain their viewpoint, held to their refusal to pay.

"It's absurd to push the question," warned one U.N. diplomat. "Trying to compel the Soviet Union to contribute to an action intended to thwart its interests in Africa would be like expecting the United States to contribute to the support of Castro. The American case is legal but unrealistic. If Washington keeps pressing its demands, the General Assembly may simply have to suspend operations. End of the U.N.!"

The American delegation persisted, nevertheless, until three years later President Lyndon Johnson abandoned the effort, in the hope of getting negotiations started with Moscow on the international control of nuclear arms.

When nothing, as usual, came out of Tshombe's evasive talks with Adoula and the U.N., he returned to Elizabethville in an ebullient mood. Convinced that his position had strengthened while Adoula's power had weakened, he ordered his troops to resume harassing U.N. forces in Katanga.

For four days the U.N. withstood Katangan fire without returning it, because U Thant shared Hammarskjöld's repugnance for the use of force to achieve unification of the Congo. But on December 29, 1962, the new Secretary General reluctantly ordered Indian Brigadier General Reginald Noronha to use his U.N. troops to crush Tshombe once and for all.

When Noronha led armored columns in a full-scale attack, Katangan forces scattered before them like matchsticks. Tshombe threatened to blow up all of Union Miniere's mining installations and leave the Central Government nothing but scorched earth and rubble. But by January 15 his mercenaries were in full retreat.

Tshombe's threat backfired. Whole towns surrendered to the U.N. forces without firing a shot, preferring U.N. protection to Tshombe's bluster about total destruction. His regime, in collapse, proved such a paper tiger that, ironically, it won him new recognition as a remarkably shrewd politician. Who else could have defied and held off the forces of the whole world so long by sheer ingenious bluff?

Surrendering after a resistance of only three weeks, the incredible Tshombe then blithely insisted on throwing a gala banquet for his conqueror, General Noronha. At the reception, still scheming mischief, Tshombe hinted to Noronha to beware of trusting his U.N. superiors. White Belgians had promised full support for Tshombe's resistance, then let him down.

"Watch out for these whites!" he warned the Indian commander darkly. "They are *your* worst enemies, too."

But whatever crafty wild new scheme he may have had in

mind did him no good with Noronha. Tshombe was forced to flee, taking sanctuary in Salisbury, Rhodesia.

Despite agonizing setbacks, the U.N. intervention had at long last restored the authority of the Congo Republic without provoking a Soviet-American clash in the heart of Africa. This accomplishment, however, only further embittered the U.N.'s conservative critics in the United States.

"We have seen the inexplicable and disgusting episode in the Congo," said Senator Barry Goldwater, "when the United Nations, financed by $40 million of U.S. money, brought war into Katanga, the one part of the Congo where there was peace and a growing prosperity, and insisted that the government there submit to a Communist-dominated central authority."

All was still far from serene in the chaotic Congo. The A.N.C. army still remained as brutal and undisciplined as when it had been the Force Publique of Belgian colonial days. Burning villages, the A.N.C. indulged in mass slaughter and put entire tribes to flight. Only 2,000 of Tshombe's gendarmes were absorbed into its ranks. Another 15,000 melted away with their weapons, nursing a bitter score to settle.

By the end of January, 1963, however, Baluba refugees began returning to their homes; the U.N. began withdrawing troops; and Joseph Ileo went to Katanga to direct the integration of the recaptured province with the Central Government.

In the spring Adoula announced the formation of a new "government of national reconciliation." The reconciliation was something less than overwhelming, with Gizenga still in jail, Tshombe and Gbenye fled, and Sendwe dropped from the Cabinet as a minister.

Long-suffering teachers of the Congo went out on strike in May, 1963. Despite almost two years of civil war, tribal fighting, massacres and army rebellions, they had stuck to their posts, often without pay. Adoula quickly agreed to pay all back salaries. UNESCO helped get the Congo's educational system working again by crash-training Congolese in school administration to fill posts in the Ministry of Education.

Strong tribal and regional pressures were put upon Adoula to carry out the Tananarive Conference resolution to divide up the Congo into 26 largely autonomous provinces. Adoula yielded and granted each new state a $4 million annual budget. The results were disastrous.

Corrupt politicians quickly plundered the province treasuries. In some governments the state capital was no more than a grocery store without electricity, telephones or water. Real power reverted to local tribal chiefs, who could now afford modern weapons for tribal warfare. Many passed laws under which tribal or political rivals were arrested for "improper behavior." Thus Tshombe's plan bore its bitter fruit even after its author had been discredited and overthrown.

Broken in health, largely friendless and despised in most of Africa as a "white man's black man," Tshombe left for Europe on June 14, 1963, as a political exile. But few Western capitals cared to have him as a resident, despite his large private fortune salted away in Swiss banks. After receiving medical care in a Paris hospital, he was finally offered sanctuary by Spanish dictator Francisco Franco.

From a Madrid office suite and a luxurious villa, Tshombe set about scheming to regain his lost power in the Congo. He had reason for optimism. Economic paralysis in the fragmented Republic had produced soaring inflation, with most

Congolese unable to afford even bread. To control mounting unrest, Mobutu had doubled the ranks of the A.N.C. only to have three new army mutinies break out.

Kasavubu and Mobutu sped to Camp Leopold to try to quiet things down, but the troops mobbed them. Beaten and almost killed, they fled in terror. Political rivals of Kasavubu sought to oust him as President. On September 29 he silenced his opposition by shutting down Parliament.

Led by Christophe Gbenye, most politicians fled across the river to Brazzaville. With the cooperation of the Congo-Brazzaville Government they set up a National Liberation Committee (C.N.L.). A mutiny in Stanleyville, engineered by the C.N.L., put a revolutionary regime there in power. Gbenye was summoned from Brazzaville to head it as "Chief of State."

His regime proved to be a bloodthirsty one, dedicated to the assassination of "counterrevolutionaries" and "American agents." Over 20,000 "traitors" were executed in grotesquely cruel fashion in front of a monument erected to Lumumba.

Gbenye's revolutionary regime represented little more than a changing of the guard from old to new scoundrels. The new officials and army officers were soon enjoying luxurious homes and privileges, while the masses they controlled continued to live in misery and hunger. The only competent official was Thomas Kanza, who joined the Stanleyville Cabinet as Foreign Minister in October. Horrified by the executions, he left in disgust after three days in office.

Adoula appealed to the West for help. Belgium signed an economic pact with the Central Government, promising a billion-dollar investment and technical assistance. Washington rushed aid and advisers when Adoula accused Gbenye and the C.N.L. of receiving arms from the Soviet Union and Red China.

Chinese Prime Minister Chou-En-lai, touring Africa in December, declared in obvious satisfaction, "An excellent revolutionary situation exists." Anti-Government uprisings had broken out in new Kwilu Province in the west, led by Pierre Mulele, a Congolese trained in Red China.

His forces were Bapende and Babunda tribesmen trained in guerrilla fighting. They blew up bridges, sank ferries, destroyed vehicles, assassinated rival politicians and drove out whites. Mulele assured his followers that as long as they were loyal to him, they were indestructible. "Bullets can only kill traitors," he explained, adding that they were fighting to protect a magic Golden Book containing all the powerful secrets of the Congo.

"It was given by Lumumba to Gizenga," he told them, "and smuggled out of jail by Gizenga to me."

On January 21, 1964, Kasavubu was forced to declare a state of emergency in Kwilu. Mulele's rebellion spread to Kivu, then to northern Katanga. Government troops were frequently driven off by daring young guerrillas armed only with bows and arrows. About a fourth of the Congo, including most of the large towns, fell into the hands of the rebels.

Adoula's prestige sank rapidly. The threat of rebellion loomed large in Leopoldville itself, where a plot to assassinate both Kasavubu and Adoula came to light.

Adoula did not dare send any more A.N.C. troops against the rebels because he distrusted their loyalty. Moreover, undependable or not, they were all he could rely upon to thwart attempts to overthrow or assassinate him.

The helplessness of Adoula, Kasavubu and Mobutu to cope

with Mulele, Gbenye and other rebels made many Congolese
leaders feel that the only hope for the country now lay in a
new government under that wily politician who had proved
the most adroit of them all, despite his defeat. Former supporters and rivals, including General Joseph Mobutu himself,
found their way to his headquarters in Madrid.

Tshombe was already busy organizing mercenaries and
his old gendarmerie into a new private army. The Portuguese
had agreed to let him station his forces on the Angola side
of the Katanga border. But in secret negotiations Mobutu convinced him that he might be able to take a more direct route
back to power through Leopoldville. Not just as Premier of
Katanga this time, but of the whole Congo!

Tshombe was enthralled by the prospect. But he knew that
to topple Adoula he would need the support not only of the
Central Government's right-wing enemies, but also of the left
—Gizenga, Gbenye, Mulele. To have any hope of winning
them over, he would have to cleanse himself of the stigma of
Lumumba's murder, and of being a Belgian stooge.

So Tshombe cleverly planted his "confessions" in a leading Belgian newspaper. He "revealed" that Lumumba had,
indeed, been foully murdered as the result of a plot by
Adoula, but that he himself had been innocent. Africans were
skeptical until the Belgian Government lent credulity to his
"exposé" by suppressing the paper that had printed it.

Tshombe then shrewdly denounced both the Belgians and
Americans for their interference in Congo affairs. He defended Gbenye and Mulele as "honest patriots driven to rebellion
out of frustration," and demanded Gizenga's release from
jail. In another amazing about-face, he began paying visits

with unashamed aplomb to nationalistic African leaders, seeing to erase his old image as "the white man's black man."

Backed by his personal fortune, Tshombe's brazen projection of himself as an African nationalist was shrewdly successful in blurring the memory of him as an unscrupulous tool of colonialism, a ruthless politician whose sabotage of national unity had brought the Congo to ruin.

Kasavubu, no fool, smelled a coup d'etat in the wind. Aware of Mobutu's visit to Madrid, he nevertheless felt personally secure because Tshombe's "confessions" had carefully spared him from any blame for Lumumba's murder.

In another incredible twist of the already tortuously convoluted Congo story, Kasavubu reached a stunning decision. He cabled the "traitor of Katanga," whom he had once jailed for treason, that their country now needed his great patriotic services. Tshombe was invited to return to the Congo to form a new transitional government of "national unity."

Adoula was finished, Kasavubu knew, because of his inability to defeat the rebels and restore national order. Tshombe's clever espousal of Gizenga, Gbenye and Mulele would win their support of him as Prime Minister, and end the rebellion. Gizenga's release from jail and cabinet portfolio would neutralize Soviet and Red Chinese opposition. Tshombe's paratroop mercenaries would also bring the A.N.C. to heel.

So on June 26, 1964, tremendous crowds in Leopoldville cheered the triumphant return of Moise Tshombe from exile to take power in the Republic he had tried to destroy.

# 14
# Paratroop Rescue

HE WAS DRIVEN FROM THE AIRPORT through a ten-mile corri-
dor of enthusiastic Congolese who shrieked their acclaim.
Standing up in the car, the dapper leader grinned his ac-
knowledgement of a hero's welcome. When he was greeted by
Kasavubu, the two men embraced like the fondest of friends.

Taking over Adoula's portfolio, Tshombe quickly set about
reconciling as many dissident elements in the Congo as possible. He visited Stanleyville to lay a wreath at the monument erected to Lumumba. Gizenga was released from jail
after two and a half years of imprisonment. Albert Kalonji
was invited to return from European exile to the Cabinet.

But many Congolese leaders were stunned by Tshombe's
incredible comeback. How could yesterday's outcast and
traitor be today's Prime Minister? It was as though following
America's Civil War, Jefferson Davis had been elected President of the United States.

Suspicious black politicians noted that the new Tshombe
regime was provided with U.S. military transports and pilots
to move his troops from one trouble spot to another to crush
resistance where rebels refused to lay down their arms. Had

164

Tshombe's return been secretly manipulated by the U.S. State Department, through the CIA, to win a "slice of cake" in Katanga? How else explain the sudden elevation to power of an unscrupulous politician, crony of the mining interests, who was despised by most Africans as a traitor to both his country and the cause of black nationalism?

The role of the CIA behind the scenes was a moot question, but Tshombe's own resourcefulness in returning to power could not be denied. A consummate and skilled politician who recognized no permanent allegiance to any cause or country, he had only one unchanging goal—personal power.

Highly adaptable, capable, ruthless and an effective leader, he knew how to advance and retreat with the tide of events. Tshombe was basically a political mercenary—for sale to the highest bidder capable of keeping him in power. His lack of scruples, noted the *New Republic*, was mistaken for a policy: "He is not pro-colonial, not pro-white, not pro-Belgian. . . . No ideology ever interferes with his opportunism."

Now it was in his hands that the fate of the Congo lay as the last of the U.N. forces withdrew on June 30, 1964.

It was more than time, U Thant felt, that the four-year-old Republic begin to look after its own security. But the U.N., with substantial help from Washington, had to continue providing technicians, educators, administrators and police instructors to stabilize the Central Government.

"Many difficulties attended the United Nations effort in the Congo," Senator Eugene McCarthy said in summing up the intervention, "and its performance has been much criticized. Yet, considering that this was the first effort at peacekeeping on such a scale . . . and also that the organization

165

was largely unprepared for a test of such magnitude, it did very well."

The opposition to Tshombe quickly boiled to a head when he made it clear that he would not "coerce" Katanga to submit to federal power. Gizenga, only two days out of jail, denounced the new administration and was promptly rejailed.

A.N.C. troops learned that Tshombe had ordered a battalion of commandos to be trained by white mercenaries as an elite corps for Mobutu and himself. Outraged at what they considered an insult to government forces, and a clear sign of distrust, many A.N.C. units rebelled. They joined Gizenga followers in capturing Stanleyville and setting up a breakaway People's Republic of the Congo. Communist block nations quickly recognized their regime and rushed aid.

Two weeks later Tshombe sent mercenaries to attack Bukava, capital of rebel-held Kivu. They were supported by CIA-trained Cuban pilots flying American rocket-firing planes. The mercenaries took no prisoners, slaughtering everyone in sight. Over 1,000 Congolese were killed at Bukavu.

Thousands of new mercenaries were flocking to Leopoldville in response to Tshombe's ads in South Africa and Rhodesia, offering high pay for "employment with a difference." White racists, ex-Nazis, French Foreign Legionnaires, white slavers, professional soldiers, adventurers, sadists, criminals and anti-Communist fanatics made up the professional killers who were hired by the Central Government.

Some fought naked to the waist, others in pirate garb or jungle coveralls, as they massacred Tshombe's opponents. In the northeast Gbenye's forces were sent reeling. On September 2 he sent U Thant an angry warning that Stanleyville was holding as hostages 1,300 whites from 25 different countries.

Five days later Belgium signed a new agreement with Tshombe promising increased military aid. The United States also turned over to him 344 vehicles and 31 planes, including three B-26 bombers complete with CIA-trained crews. President Lyndon B. Johnson, who had previously expressed admiration for Tshombe's fight as a secessionist, now affirmed a desire to help him succeed as Prime Minister of the Congo.

Other African nations once more accused Tshombe of being a colonial puppet. Tshombe charged Gizenga and Gbenye with being Communist stooges. In September a worried meeting of the Organization of African Unity (O.A.U.) at Addis Ababa called upon both sides to reject foreign aid and stop fighting. It was obvious that the Cold War had filled the vacuum left by the departure of the U.N. forces.

A conference of nonaligned countries was held in Cairo a month later. Tshombe flew there uninvited, hoping to win support for his regime. Egypt's Colonel Gamal Nasser angrily put him under house arrest until the conference was over. Freed after four days, Tshombe returned to Leopoldville full of dire warnings about the threat of "Arab imperialism."

Both Washington and Brussels were deeply worried about the fate of the 1,300 white Westerners held as hostages by Gbenye in Stanleyville. Persistent negotiations failed to win their freedom because Gbenye regarded their presence as his only protection against an all-out attack on Stanleyville.

Tshombe ignored all attempts by the Western powers to restrain him. If he could provoke Gbenye into killing hostages, Washington and Brussels would be infuriated into wiping out the rebels instantly. So his planes pounded towns

in Oriental Province to rubble, while his ground forces overran and destroyed others with blazing tank guns.

Embittered rebels who fled those towns left behind, with
their own casualties, whites and blacks executed in reprisal
as "enemies of the revolution." Tshombe's mercenaries and
A.N.C. troops looted every village they captured, and con-
ducted mass executions of suspected rebels.

"They didn't put up any fight," one mercenary reported at
Kindu. "We just killed until, by the time it was dark, we
thought there was nobody left alive."

Some prisoners were crowded into canoes and machine-
gunned. Then these cargoes of death were floated downstream,
along with surplus bodies flung into the currents of the Lulu-
aba River, as a ghastly warning to Stanleyville's defenders.

On October 5, Gbenye's capital fell under siege. He grew
hysterical with rage and fear. When water and food began
to run low, he broadcast a threat to kill every white hostage
in his hands if Tshombe did not end the assault.

"In the name of Lumumba," he cried. "I utter a last appeal!" When Tshombe's forces pressed on, Gbenye couldn't
bring himself to carry out his threat. But his rhetoric had
inflamed the besieged rebels to a point beyond his control.

In Stanleyville and other towns of Oriental Province, enraged Congolese dragged captive whites to public squares for
swift "trial." Forced to swallow gasoline, victims were set
afire until their bodies exploded.

To bring about a truce and free the hostages, the O.A.U.
set up a ten-nation Congo Conciliation Commission headed by
Prime Minister Jomo Kenyatta of Kenya. Tshombe agreed to
cooperate with the commission, but warned he would brook
no interference in Congo's internal affairs.

He was outraged on September 22 when Kenyatta appealed to the United States to end all military aid to Tshombe. Kasavubu denounced Kenyatta and the O.A.U. for "manifest interference." Washington and Brussels decided that Kenyatta's efforts to rescue the hostages were too slow and uncertain.

They secretly collaborated on their own plan for a crash rescue mission. Gbenye learned that U.S. Air Force planes were flying Belgian paratroops into the Kamina air base in Katanga. He promptly sought to "tighten security" by arresting Stanleyville's mayor, along with 99 other suspected "enemies of the revolution" who had listened to Tshombe's broadcasts. All were machine-gunned in front of Lumumba's monument.

Then Gbenye made an impassioned broadcast warning that if the city were attacked from the air, all remaining hostages would be slaughtered immediately. And he threatened any "imperialist aggressors" who dared enter Stanleyville: "We will wear the hearts of Belgians and Americans as fetishes —and we will dress in their skins!"

On November 24, U.S. Air Force planes flew over the rebel capital. A blood-red dawn sky blossomed with the billowing chutes of 600 Belgian paratroops swaying toward earth.

In those same dramatic moments 250 white hostages were driven into the streets as Radio Stanleyville blared, "Kill them all—men, women and children!"

Simbas clad in monkey fur manes opened fire with rifles and Sten guns. Agonized parents sought to shield children's bodies with their own. Many hostages fled, but 29 were gunned down. One of those killed was a well-known American medical missionary, Dr. Paul E. Carlson.

Tumbling to the ground, the paratroops struggled to free

themselves from their shrouds. Then they tore into the Simbas, machine guns blazing. After only brief resistance, the natives scattered into the bush. Some hours later a Congolese Army brigade, led by 300 white mercenaries, reached the city and reinforced the paratroops. As Stanleyville fell, Gbenye and his rebel Cabinet fled with almost $800,000 in gold.

The mercenaries pressed on to adjacent towns. At Paul they found 51 white bodies savagely hacked and cannibalized. White hostages who had survived reported that they had been treated decently at first, but were beaten and abused when the American planes began bombing the town.

The commandos were able to rescue 1,300 white people of 17 nationalities, including 55 Americans. Tshombe greeted the first group of rescued hostages as they arrived in Leopold-ville on 40 U.S. transport planes. Many came off on stretchers.

The success of the rescue mission, and the occupation of Stanleyville by Tshombe's forces, ended the rebellion in Oriental Province. But the victory proved costly. Enraged Simbas tortured and slaughtered both whites and pro-Tshombe blacks. By the end of November over 12,000 Africans, including the best-educated Congolese of Oriental Province, had been slain. Thousands had been killed indiscriminately by the mercenaries, who took no prisoners.

"You just kill anything black in front of you," one mercenary shrugged. "You can't risk trying to sort out the good guys from the bad guys. It isn't practical."

Tshombe's A.N.C. troops were equally ruthless. Occupying Stanleyville, they rounded up 20,000 natives as military and political prisoners. The captives were taken to a local sports arena to be "tried" by a mob of spectators. Prisoners cheered were released; those hooted were shot and thrown in the river.

The Western press largely ignored the atrocities committed against Congolese by Tshombe's mercenaries and A.N.C. troops, stressing only those against white nuns and missionaries committed by black rebels.

A hot debate broke out in the U.N. Security Council.

"The United States," challenged the delegate from Ghana, "is no more entitled to intervention than would, say, Ghana be entitled to intervention in the Southern states of the United States of America to protect lives of Afro-American inhabitants of those states, who are, from time to time, tortured and murdered for asserting their legitimate rights."

The American delegate repeated President Johnson's defense of the rescue operation as purely a mission of mercy made necessary by African savagery. But cynical African delegates saw the intervention primarily as a Western blow in the Cold War designed to knock out the Congo's pro-Communist faction.

The Sudanese delegate reminded the council caustically that after U.N. forces had labored so long and painfully to get the mercenaries out of the Congo, Brussels and Washington had brought them back again in even greater numbers. How could that be justified as a "peace-keeping" operation?

Other delegates charged that the rescue operation had provoked, not prevented, the violence that followed. The Belgian-American plan was also accused of having cynically sabotaged Kenyatta's negotiations to secure peaceful release of the hostages.

Why, challenged some African delegates, was the brutal killing of 80 whites so much more deplorable than the murder of thousands of Congolese by the mercenaries? If the killing of 80 whites represented a "reversion by Africans to

171

savagery," what should be said about a white colonialism in Africa that had been responsible for the deaths of millions of blacks?

From London, Conor Cruise O'Brien raised another embarrassing question: "Are white people in Africa to be regarded as covered by a sort of Caucasian providence insurance policy, with a guarantee that if the natives get rough, the metropolitan forces will once again come to the rescue?"

The paratroop mission should be condemned by the U.N. as an illegal act, O'Brien insisted. Otherwise every free African nation would be completely justified in excluding all whites from its territory, in order to avoid the risk of similar violation of its sovereignty.

Washington argued that the rescue mission was legal because it had had the consent of the legal government of the Congo, while Communist bloc shipments of arms to the rebels were illegal. The U.N.'s pan-African bloc replied tartly that Tshombe ruled only by virtue of the guns of his white mercenaries and support of Western capitalists, not by approval of the Congo Parliament.

The storm aroused by the rescue mission reverberated around the world. In Djakarta, Indonesia, mobs of youths smashed windows and doors of the U.S. Information Service Library, forcing it to shut down. Anti-American riots took place in Egypt and Algeria.

Early in December planeloads of arms and ammunition were flown by Algeria, Egypt and Ghana to secret rebel strongholds. Other supplies arrived by ship from East Germany and Red China. Tshombe learned that Watusi warriors and former Mau Mau guerrillas of Kenya were being recruited by the rebels to help drive the mercenaries out of the Congo.

Tshombe grew worried. He felt that he would need a bigger, better-equipped mercenary army to keep his power. After the uproar over the rescue mission, he could hardly look to Washington or Belgium for that support. So he flew to Europe in search of the new money and equipment he needed.

Left-wing riots in Rome doomed his mission there. He encountered less trouble when he flew to Paris to see De Gaulle, who agreed to help train the A.N.C. army, as well as provide teachers, administrative exports and investment capital.

The Belgians, worried about French rivalry for control of the Congo's great mineral resources, ordered Tshombe to cancel the French deal. He coldly replied that if they tried to stop it, he would nationalize Union Miniere.

The Belgians quickly backed down.

As one correspondent saw him at this time, Tshombe had developed into a ruthless, polished actor who could charm an aide one moment and fire him the next. Concentrating all power in his own hands, because he trusted no one, he was compelled to sign mountains of documents daily. U.N. officials complained that he signed them without reading them, often issuing decrees on Tuesday that contradicted those he had signed on Monday.

He was hurt because most leaders of other African nations refused to have anything to do with him. "If I am strong," he insisted wistfully, "they will eventually be forced to accept me."

One African ambassador to the Congo criticized him for employing too many white Europeans in his administration.

They were necessary evils, he pleaded. Besides, he had made sure that they came from many different nations, so that they would spy on one another and keep him informed of everything that was going on.

In May, 1965, Tshombe sought to win respectability for his regime by joining O.C.A.M., an organization of 14 French-speaking African states. They included mostly politically moderate countries like the Ivory Coast, Niger and Dahomey. When Tshombe strode into the crowded O.C.A.M. conference hall at Abidjan, delegates rose, applauded and cried, *"Vive Tshombe!"*

He was astonished and delighted to find himself hailed as an important African statesman, instead of a former secessionist, alleged murderer of Lumumba, "white man's black man" in Africa or employer of brutal white mercenaries.

At a press conference afterward he was asked about the status of the Congo rebels. "We no longer have a problem of rebellion in the Congo," he replied blithely. "At the present time our most important problem is mopping up the few groups who have been supported by certain African countries and certain other foreign countries."

He did succeed in crushing the rebellion by September, 1965. Gbenye fled to Cairo in a Rolls Royce. Temporarily the Congo had been restored to peace, but it was a peace that smelled of the graveyard. Plantations were abandoned. Palm oil, cotton and diamond industries had been badly crippled.

Roads, bridges and communications were a shambles. Only Union Miniere operations had, significantly, been left untouched. There was a serious shortage of teachers, government clerks, postmasters and civil servants. The 200,000 Congolese who had lost their lives since Independence Day included the most educated Congolese, executed by rebels as "reactionaries."

The rebellion over, Kasavubu considered that Tshombe had served the purpose for which he had been called out of exile. "King Kasa" had no intention of allowing the ebullient Prime Minister to make himself dictator of the Congo.

On October 13, 1965, Kasavubu fired Tshombe and named BALUBAKAT's Evariste Kimba as the new Prime Minister.

Stunned, Tshombe quickly rallied his own supporters by promising them glowing rewards. They persuaded Parliament to reject Kimba and continue Tshombe in office. What happened next made many Congolese, as well as foreign correspondents, sigh, "This is where we came in!"

Once more, in a bloodless coup, General Joseph Mobutu stepped forward to seize power for himself.

# 15

# "Please Leave the Congo Alone!"

HE WOULD GOVERN THE CONGO without elections for five years, he announced. Reluctant agreement came from Parliament, which did not see how it could quarrel with Mobutu's troops. Besides, some politicians argued, dictatorship was preferable to having the country once more torn apart in a new struggle for power between Tshombe and Kasavubu.

Fearing a new plot to assassinate him, Tshombe fled into exile once more. But the Communist bloc allied to Red China denounced Mobutu and swore to overthrow him. On December 28, 1965, Radio Peking announced it would continue to support 20,000 rebels fighting in Kivu. Red China was still pursuing the goal visualized by Mao Tse-tung when he declared, "If we take the Congo, we shall hold the whole of Africa."

In February, 1966, Gizenga was freed and fled to Brazzaville, where the Republic of Congo (Brazzaville) had become the chief base for Red Chinese penetration of Africa.

Tshombe strove to unseat Mobutu from exile. The dictator found his new control of the Congo shaky. Belgium reneged on all financial arrangements made with Tshombe. Unpaid white mercenaries and pro-Tshombe A.N.C. units rebelled.

In March, Mobutu sentenced Tshombe to death in absentia for "treason and conspiracy." Four ex-ministers, including Evariste Kimba, were hung for plotting to kill Mobutu. In October, Mobutu fired a new Prime Minister he had appointed, for plotting an army mutiny against him in Katanga.

As though to change the complexion of the turbulent country he sought to subdue, on July 1, 1966, Mobutu renamed Leopoldville Kinshasa; Stanleyville became Kisangani; Elizabethville was transformed into Lumbashi.

In December he struck back at Belgium for refusing to support him by canceling all of Union Miniere's concessions and seizing its assets for the Central Government.

Dismissing Parliament, he replaced it with his own one-house legislature. Then he rammed through a new constitution that allowed him to rule by decree. It also consolidated the provinces into a total of eight, plus the new capital district of Kinshasa (Leopoldville). To curb tribalism and nepotism, and weaken anti-Government plotting, Mobutu forbade any province to be governed by officials from that region.

Under strong man Mobutu, the Congo was anything but the democracy it was alleged to be. But he claimed credit for bringing at least a temporary halt to the turmoil and chaos that had agonized the Republic since its birth.

On June 29, 1967, Tshombe, once more a refugee in Spain, boarded a flight from Mallorca to Barcelona. In midair the plane was hijacked at gunpoint by one of his own mercenary bodyguards, and ordered to fly to Algiers. The hijacker's motive was unclear, but journalists suggested that as a mercenary he had simply sold out to Mobutu for more money.

In Algiers, Tshombe was held in detention, but Algeria's President Houari Boumedienne refused to turn him over to Mobutu as a "war criminal." Boumedienne's pretext was that the Algerian Constitution forbade extradition of a refugee for political offenses; but his real price for delivering up Tshombe was Mobutu's agreement to break relations with Israel. Mobutu had invited military instructors from Tel Aviv to train his parachute regiment.

When Mobutu rejected Boumedienne's secret offer, Tshombe languished moodily in solitary confinement in Algeria. His agents' appeals to Brussels, Paris and Washington to rescue him by diplomacy or muscle went ignored.

Meanwhile, Belgian and French mercenaries had organized a rebellion against government forces in the eastern Congo. Washington sent three large U.S. transport planes to help Mobutu fly troops and supplies to his A.N.C. forces in the trouble spots. *The Nation* reported that behind this move were American financial interests seeking Mobutu's approval of their 40 per cent investment in a new Congolese company.

In July, 1968, Boumedíenne suddenly announced that the 40-year-old Tshombe had died of a heart attack in a ten-room villa on the outskirts of Algiers. To dispel any suspicion that he had been murdered like Lumumba, Boumedíenne produced a death certificate signed by 12 physicians.

But African skeptics believed that Mobutu's long arm, which had already murdered another exile fleeing his retribution, Pierre Mulele, had now reached out to slay Tshombe.

By a curious coincidence, Tshombe's death had come on the eve of the Congo's ninth anniversary of independence. And it had occurred only three weeks before he had been scheduled to be freed, through the negotiations of lawyers hired by his wife in New York. He was buried not in his native land, Algeria or Spain, but in a suburban cemetery in Brussels.

His heart, some critics alleged caustically, had always been there. To most Africans, Tshombe was still the "white man's black man," protecting the imperialist wealth of Katanga with brutal white mercenaries.

His obituaries recalled a cartoon Bill Mauldin had drawn showing a pith-helmeted Senator James Eastland, Mississippi's champion of white supremacy, greeting a grinning African in the jungle by inquiring with hopeful anxiety, "Mr. Tshombe, I presume?"

But Tshombe was not without mourners who saw him as a symbol of Christian anti-Communism in Africa, a skillful leader willing to utilize white help in "bringing his people out of darkest savagery." To conservatives he had been the only respectable answer to black revolution.

"He was convinced that the progress of his country and of Africa could be achieved," observed the right-wing *National Review*, "only through the cooperation of black with white, and the aid of white expertise and capital. . . . He tried to save his own region of Katanga from the spreading chaos. This World Opinion would not permit." Tshombe might have been overly ambitious and hungry for power, but "he was most surely a man on any account more sinned against than sinning."

In the first five years of his authoritarian rule, General Joseph Mobutu managed to achieve relative political and economic stability in the Congo. He was able to do so, ironically, only by inviting back the white capital and management that had been driven out of the country by independence.

Tens of thousands of Belgian advisers, managers, engineers and pilots were induced to return and work for the Mobutu regime by an offer of bonus salaries. Investment capital was lured back by the offer of new liberal terms and guarantees, as well as the assurance of a stabilized currency.

In September, 1969, Mobutu worked out a settlement with Union Miniere that let the Government take over copper production, with Japanese cooperation, through a new State company called Gecomin.

Despite years of bedlam, revolt and corruption, economists still rate the Congo's chances of reaching economic self-sufficiency as among the best of any African country. A land of fabulous copper, cobalt and diamond deposits, it may soon also prove to be rich in oil as well. In addition to hydroelectric resources, it has soils and climates that can grow almost anything, and a vast system of navigable rivers to ship its profitable exports to the world.

"The Congo is a honey pot," observed one Belgian businessman fondly. "The bees may fly away for a while, but they always come back to the honey pot!"

Evidence of the bees' return was everywhere in Kinshasa in early 1970, when the former city of Leopoldville underwent an extraordinary construction boom. The suburbs were thronged with new villas, the streets with new vehicles.

Workers were restless, however, because the new boom had produced an inflation that had reduced their buying power, while once more white Belgians lived close by in great style and comfort. In the vast interior of the Congo, millions of Africans were still living almost as primitively as they had when King Leopold was running the country.

Educated young Congolese fiercely resented the lack of

democracy and free elections under Mobutu. In June, 1969, students from Lavanium University staged a protest demonstration in Kinshasa for higher educational grants. When Mobutu ordered A.N.C. troops to break up the demonstration, nine students were killed. Mobutu coolly blamed their deaths on agitation against him by "foreign embassies and troublemakers."

The seventies will undoubtedly produce new stresses and strains in the ever-turbulent Congo. How long "strong man" Mobutu will continue to hold power in a storm center that has swept away Lumumba, Adoula, Kasavubu, Kimba and Tshombe is a moot question. It is possible that he will prudently step down and permit the return of an elected government. The latest indications, however, suggest that if he does permit elections, he will seek to entrench himself in power by refusing to allow serious opposition by a rival political party.

With or without elections, his chances of survival would seem questionable in an unpredictable, unstable country with so volcanic a history in its first decade of independence.

What are some of the lessons the world—and we—might have been expected to learn from the emergence of the Congo as an independent nation?

Certainly there can be general agreement that it was a tragic blunder for the Belgians, having failed to train and prepare an educated class of Congolese for the complex responsibilities of independence, to turn the Congo loose so abruptly. Unprepared leaders had found themselves unable to operate the new republic, while faced by the unrealistic expectations of an uneducated people who expected independence automatically to bring them all their fondest dreams wrapped in shiny bright new packages.

Independence had only swept the Congolese from the frying pan of colonialism into the fire of anarchy.

When American journalist John Gunther returned from a trip to study the new republics of Africa, he was asked whether he believed that most emerging African nations had been ready for self-government. They had not been, he replied, but all were determined to govern themselves, ready or not.

"The colonial powers were no longer willing to expend the blood, sweat and money necessary to hold them down," he explained. "The tragedy is that Africa was too . . . grievously undereducated to be able to take advantage fruitfully of its new freedom. And the old empires bear a large share of responsibility for this misfortune, lamentable as it was."

Perhaps the chief lesson to be learned is that every underdeveloped nation emerging from under another country's thumb needs first to be guaranteed a *timetable* of independence. An outside time limit of, say, four or five years would allow the brightest and best-educated nationals to be trained and prepared for leadership and managerial roles, and the population to be taught what changes to expect independence to bring.

French African colonies were freed with a smooth transition to independence because the French had wisely trained 7,000 African university graduates beforehand.

The underdeveloped nations of the world also want to be allowed to develop their own institutions in their own way. Nations that help are only resented when they insist that their own examples be followed.

"Others may feel that they have evolved the very best way of life," observes Ghana's Prime Minister, "but we are not bound, like slavish imitators, to accept it as our mold. If we find the methods used by others are suitable to our social environments, we shall adopt them; if we find them unsuitable, we shall reject them."

Most world diplomats subscribe to the Hammarskjöld-U Thant conviction that no ideological conflict between great powers should be allowed to use any underdeveloped nation as the rope in a tug-of-war contest.

Mario Cardoso, once the Congo's representative at the U.N., accused Western capitalism of having provoked the secession of Katanga. He also denounced the Communist bloc nations for having fomented the secession in Oriental Province.

"It is not the Congolese that are divided," he insisted. "It is the world that is divided. Therefore, please leave the Congo alone!"

It is sobering to reflect that had it not been for the restraining influence of the U.N. intervention in the Congo, the Cold War struggle there between Washington and Moscow might possibly have escalated to a point where nuclear flames and dust clouds could have threatened all life on earth.

As America moved into the seventies, there were encouraging indications that Washington's foreign policy had moved from an era of confrontation to an era of conciliation, with corresponding moves in this direction from Moscow.

Perhaps both powers will eventually agree that world peace is endangered by the unilateral intervention by any major power in the internal affairs of developing nations. Such direct aid to an underdeveloped nation struggling for nationhood is likely to give the intervening power a vested interest in that country. If this provokes a countermove by the rival major power, the end result may be the kind of highly dangerous confrontation that upset the stability of the Congo.

Senator William Fulbright, Chairman of the Senate Foreign Relations Committee, has recommended that all military and economic aid to developing nations be channeled only through the United Nations. In that way no major power could become involved as direct creditors with an interest to protect.

Whether this or a similar plan becomes the American foreign policy of tomorrow, Secretary of State William Rogers, speaking for the Nixon Administration, has made it clear that the United States from now on will be extremely reluctant to intervene directly in the internal problems of underdeveloped nations struggling for nationhood.

Whatever the weaknesses of the United Nations, as the only peace force representing most of the nations of the world it is obviously the best choice to play the role of world policeman in keeping the peace. Since peace is in the best interests of both Moscow and Washington, perhaps they will agree to stop wasting their resources in military maneuvering against each other, and will cooperate instead in strengthening the U.N.'s ability to prevent future wars.

Our humanitarian heritage requires that we do not turn our backs on the people of underdeveloped nations who look to us for help as they struggle to emerge out of colonialism and feudalism. But we must find better ways of lifting them out of the darkness than turning them loose in a chaotic hell.

The tragedy of the Congo stands as a grim warning.

# Suggested Further Readings

Archer, Jules. *African Firebrand: Kenyatta of Kenya*. New York: Julian Messner, 1969.

Ascherson, Neal. *The King Incorporated*. Garden City, N.Y.: Doubleday & Company, 1964.

Belgian Government. *Belgian Congo* (Two Volumes). Brussels: Belgian Congo and Ruanda-Urundi Information and Public Relations Office, 1959, 1960.

Cohen, John. *Africa Addio*. New York: Ballantine Books, 1966.

Conrad, Joseph. *Heart of Darkness*. New York: Dell Publishing Co., Inc., 1960.

Gunther, John. *Inside Africa*. New York: Harper & Brothers, 1955.

Hempstone, Smith. *Rebels, Mercenaries, and Dividends*. New York: Frederick A. Praeger, Publisher, 1962.

Horn, Major General Carl von. *Soldiering for Peace*. New York: David McKay Company, 1967.

Kitchen, Helen, ed. *Footnotes to the Congo Story*. New York: Walker and Company, 1960-1967.

Lefevre, Ernest W. *Crisis in the Congo: A United Nations Force In Action*. Washington, D.C.: Brooks Institute, 1965.

Lessing, Pieter. *Africa's Red Harvest*. New York: The John Day Company, 1962.

Lumumba, Patrice. *Congo, My Country*. New York, Washington, London: Frederick A. Praeger, 1962.

Merriam, Alan P. *Congo: Background of Conflict*. Evanston, Ill.: Northwestern University Press, 1961.

O'Brien, Conor Cruise. *To Katanga and Back*. New York: Simon and Schuster, 1962.

U.S. Department of State. *Background Notes: Congo (Kinshasa)*. Washington, D.C.: U.S. Government Printing Office, 1968.

Articles and news stories on the Congo consulted for this book were found in *Christian Century, Current Biography, Look, Dublin Times, National Review, New Republic, Newsweek, The New York Times, Poughkeepsie Journal, Reader's Digest, Time, Variety, Wall Street Journal.*

# Index

# INDEX

De Gaulle, Chas., 62, 63, 126, 173
De Schrijver, Auguste, 73, 74, 80, 82, 85, 89
Dodd, Sen. T. J., 151

Eisenhower, Dwight D., 18, 98, 101, 112, 122, 128
Elections, national, 90-92
Ethiopians, 113, 125
*Evolués*, 10, 45, 46, 48-50, 52, 54, 56-58, 60-64, 68, 73, 74, 80, 81
Explorers, 25-28

Force Publique, 11, 13, 15, 18, 19, 36, 67, 68, 74, 75, 87, 88, 96, 98, 158
Franco, Francisco, 159
Fullbright, Sen. Wm., 184

Gbenye, Christopher, 155, 158, 160, 162, 163, 166-170, 174
Gecomin, 180
Ghana Conf., 66
Gheysen, Gen., 122
Gizenga, Antoine, 89, 91, 111, 113, 115, 117, 129, 132, 135, 136, 140-143, 146, 153-155, 158, 161-164, 166, 167, 176
Goldwater, Barry, 158
Gullion, Edmund, 152

Hammarskjöld, Dag, 100-106, 109, 113-123, 125, 126, 128, 129, 131, 133, 140, 142, 144-150, 157, 183

Ileo, Joseph, 53-55, 57, 59, 61, 64, 71, 127, 137, 141, 142, 144, 158
Independence Day, 11, 12, 94, 96, 175
*Inforcongo*, 62, 85
Internat. Africa Assoc., 27-31, 40
Internat. Congo Assoc., 30-32

Janssens, Gen. Emile, 13, 14, 88
Johnson, Lyndon B., 156, 167, 171

Kalonji, Albert, 64, 71, 72, 75, 76, 82, 86, 111, 120, 123, 125, 126, 140-142, 146, 154, 155, 164
Kanza, Daniel, 83
Kanza, Thomas, 50, 57, 58, 64, 110, 160
Kasavubu, Joseph, 9, 14, 16, 17, 48, 49, 52, 55, 57, 59-62, 67-71, 76-78, 82, 83, 86, 89, 91, 93-95, 97, 98, 101, 102, 104, 115, 117, 118, 126-130, 132-137, 140, 141, 144-146, 152, 160, 161, 163, 164, 169, 175, 176, 181
Katanga, 16, 18, 19, 24-26, 28, 35, 36, 39, 40, 47, 57, 59, 61, 64-66, 72, 76, 79, 82, 86, 87, 91-93, 95-99, 101, 104, 105, 107, 109, 112, 114, 116-119, 121-123, 125, 126, 128, 135-138, 140, 142-155, 157, 158, 161-163, 165, 166, 169, 177, 179, 183
Kennedy, John F., 136, 142, 152, 155
Kenyatta, Jomo, 50, 137, 168, 169, 171
Khiaria, Mahmoud, 147
Khrushchev, Nikita, 101-104, 128, 139
Kimba, Evariste, 175, 177, 181
Kitona Agreement, 152-155

Leopold II, King, 7, 26-42, 49, 180
Leopold III, King, 45
Livingstone, Dr. David, 25-28
Lumumba, Patrice, 7-9, 13, 14, 16-18, 29, 51, 52, 56, 57, 59-61, 64, 66, 67, 69-83, 86, 88-91, 94-142, 145, 146, 150, 153-156, 161-164, 169, 174, 178, 181

# INDEX

# INDEX

## About the Author

Jules Archer was born on January 27, 1915, in New York City, and attended DeWitt Clinton High School and The City College of New York. He is the author of over a thousand published articles and stories and many books for adults and young people. His work has been translated into twelve languages, reprinted by the State Department, adapted for television and included in anthologies. He has also been a consultant for the World Book Encyclopedia. The Archers live in the foothills of the Taconic Mountain Range at Pine Plains, New York. One son, Michael, a Princeton graduate, is a paleontologist. A second son, Dane, is a social scientist who graduated from Yale. A third son, Kerry, is now attending Harvard, majoring in neurological research.

N